AMERICAN BAR ASSOCIATION
Defending Liberty
Pursuing Justice

THE ETHICS OF E-DISCOVERY

John M. Barkett

FIRST CHAIR
·PRESS·

SECTION of LITIGATION
AMERICAN BAR ASSOCIATION

THE ETHICS OF E-DISCOVERY

Cover design by ABA Publishing

Printed in the United States of America.
12 11 10 09 08 5 4 3 2 1

Library of Congress Cataloging in Publication Data

Barkett, John M.
The Ethics of E-Discovery / John M. Barkett.
p. cm
ISBN 978-1-60442-256-6
1. Electronic discovery (Law)—United States. 2. Practice of law—United States—Automation. 3. Legal ethics—United States. I. Title.

KF8902.E42B39 2009
347.73′72—dc22 2008046802

Discounts are available for books ordered in bulk. Special consideration is given to state bars, CLE programs, and other bar-related organizations. Inquire at Book Publishing, ABA Publishing, American Bar Association, 321 N. Clark Street, Chicago, IL 60654.

www.ababooks.org

To Mom and Dad who taught me so much about respecting the dignity—and recognizing the needs—of others, and to Dee, John, and Leslie who are following so ably in their grandparents' footsteps.

CONTENTS

INTRODUCTION

The thorny issues associated with e-discovery were highlighted for me at the American Bar Association Section of Litigation's 2002 annual conference in Boston. There were three concurrent programs running. The first two programs I looked in on had very few attendees. The third was standing room only. A judge named Shira Scheindlin was on the panel, and this was "BZ" (before *Zubulake*[1]). I listened long enough to recognize that e-discovery would present significant ethical and malpractice concerns for all lawyers. Not much later, an e-discovery consultant confirmed my fears. He was being overwhelmed with requests to serve as an expert witness in malpractice actions against lawyers. Soon thereafter, ethics committees began to respond to e-discovery questions as well. Illustratively, one hot topic being addressed was whether it is proper for lawyers who receive electronic documents from their adversaries to mine those documents for metadata. (If you are a lawyer and you don't know what metadata is, you most certainly need to continue reading.)

Having previously written about cost-shifting and sanctions in e-discovery,[2] the prelitigation duty to preserve (which presents new challenges in the digital world where information is easily deleted and automatically recycled),[3] the December 1, 2006 "e-discovery" amendments to the federal rules of civil procedure,[4] e-discovery in

---

[1] Zubulake v. UBS Warburg LLC, 217 F.R.D. 309 (S.D.N.Y. 2003) (*Zubulake I*) (establishing cost-shifting standards). In her *Zubulake* decisions, Judge Scheindlin covered standards for cost-shifting, sampling of backup tapes, shifting of costs in part to a requesting party, the consequences of a failure to preserve backup tapes, and the standards for imposition of an adverse inference instruction resulting from spoliation of electronically stored information. In addition to *Zubulake I* and *Zubulake II* (not related to e-discovery), see Zubulake v. UBS Warburg LLC, 216 F.R.D. 280 (S.D.N.Y. 2003) (*Zubulake III*) (shifting 25 percent of the cost of production to the requesting party); Zubulake v. UBS Warburg LLC, 220 F.R.D. 212 (S.D.N.Y. 2003) (*Zubulake IV*) (finding a prelitigation duty to preserve but deciding not to impose sanctions for the prelitigation loss of electronic documents); Zubulake v. UBS Warburg LLC, 2004 U.S. Dist. LEXIS 13574 (S.D.N.Y. July 20, 2004) (*Zubulake V*) (imposing sanction of an adverse inference instruction for failure to preserve electronic information).

[2] *Bytes, Bits and Bucks: Cost-Shifting and Sanctions in E-Discovery*, ABA Section of Litigation Annual Meeting (2004) and 71 Def. Couns. J. 334 (2004).

[3] *The Prelitigation Duty to Preserve: Lookout!*, ABA Annual Meeting (Chicago 2005).

[4] *Help Is On The Way . . . Sort Of: How the Civil Rules Advisory Committee Hopes to Fill the E-Discovery Void*, ABA Section of Litigation Annual Meeting (Los Angeles 2006); *Help Has Arrived . . . Sort Of: The New E-Discovery Rules*, ABA Section of Litigation Annual Meeting (San Antonio 2007); *The Battle For Bytes: New Rule 26, "e-Discovery,"* Section of

arbitration,[5] and most recently, a potpourri of e-discovery topics,[6] I now continue this litany of work by focusing on a number of ethical issues associated with e-discovery. I will refer primarily to the American Bar Association's Model Rules of Professional Conduct (Model Rules).[7] However, I have this word of caution: While many state rules of professional conduct (RPC) are identical to the Model Rules, readers must evaluate the specific rules applicable to their professional conduct in a particular matter. The relevant state's RPC may vary from the Model Rules in ways that materially affect the lawyer's obligations.

In the spirit of Model Rule 1.1, which focuses on competence to handle a matter and emphasizes training and continuing legal education, I begin with a brief e-discovery tutorial.

LITIGATION (February 2006); *A Primer on the New Rules of E-Discovery*, 21 N.R.E. 58 (Summer 2006).

[5] *E-Discovery For Arbitrators*, 1 DISP. RES. INT'L J. 129 (December 2007).

[6] Barkett, *E-Discovery: Twenty Questions and Answers* (First Chair Press, Chicago 2008). This work covers a number of subjects about which I lectured in a law school workshop entitled "E-Discovery" at the University of Miami in the fall 2007 semester.

[7] The 2002 edition of the Model Rules reflects the work of the Commission on Evaluation of the Rules of Professional Conduct (Ethics 2000 Commission). The commission's report is cited as AMERICAN BAR ASSOCIATION, COMMISSION ON EVALUATION OF THE RULES OF PROFESSIONAL CONDUCT, REPORT WITH RECOMMENDATION TO THE HOUSE OF DELEGATES (August 2001). The Ethics 2000 Report can be downloaded at: http://www.abanet.org/cpr/e2k/e2k-report_home.html. During the August 6–7, 2001, meeting of the American Bar Association House of Delegates, the house considered the changes to the Model Rules proposed by the Ethics 2000 Commission. The house voted on the rules through Rule 1.10, and approved the commission's recommendations with certain exceptions discussed at http://www.abanet.org/cpr/e2k/e2k-summary_2002.html. At the ABA's Midyear Meeting in February 2002, the House of Delegates reviewed the remaining proposed revisions from Rule 1.11 through Rule 8.5. Its approved "Report 401" contains all of the accepted revisions to the Model Rules of Professional Conduct. *Id.* Copies of the 2008 Model Rules of Professional Conduct can be obtained through the ABA Service Center (800-285-2221; PC# 215-0023). Changes to Model Rule 5.5 (regarding the unauthorized practice of law) and 8.5 (regarding disciplinary authority and choice-of-law issues) were not included in the debate over Report 401 because the ABA Commission on Multijurisdictional Practice (CMP) was reviewing those rules as part of a separate study. *See* http://www.abanet.org/cpr/mjp/home.html to obtain the Final Report of the CMP. Rules 5.5 and 8.5 were adopted by the ABA House of Delegates in August 2002. Rules 1.6 and 1.13 were amended in August 2003. Rule 7.2 was further amended in August 2002. Rule 3.8 was amended in February 2008. The Comment to Rule 7.5 was amended in August 2002. The Comment to Rule 5.5 was amended in February 2007. *See also* A Legislative History: The Development of the ABA Model Rules of Professional Conduct, 1982-2005. PC# 215-0014.

CHAPTER ONE

Why Electronically Stored Information Is Different from Paper

The digital world differs materially from the paper world.

Everyone Is a File Keeper

In the paper world, documents typically are given to administrative staff for filing. In the digital world, every computer user who sends or receives e-mail, creates word-processing documents, prepares spreadsheets or information slides, or maintains databases decides whether to store files and has the ability to modify or delete a file. Even if the digital file keeper takes no action, it is likely that e-mail or other digital documents eventually will be moved to a backup tape that in many cases will be overwritten after some time period, causing the file to be lost forever.[1]

[1] An individual user can archive an e-mail in local storage media, and that may be the only place to find a document. *See* Hynix Semiconductor Inc., et al. v. Rambus Inc., 2006 U.S. Dist. LEXIS 30690, *27-28 (N.D. Calif. Jan. 5, 2006) (explaining that Rambus changed to a backup recycling schedule of three months and that employees should create their own

In the paper world, when an employee leaves a job, his documents, already archived, may remain in that state until a records-retention schedule calls for their destruction. In the digital world, when an employee leaves a job, her desktop or laptop hard drive (or both) may be reformatted, destroying all data on the drive(s) unless someone decides that there are litigation or business reasons to maintain the employee's digital status quo.[2]

In the paper world, when, say, a major construction project was completed, the paper associated with the project might be boxed and stored in a warehouse. In the digital world, the desktop and laptop computers used by everyone in the field may be moved to the next job. File management may be a function of project organization, or perhaps serendipity, depending on the individual file-keeping habits of each person on the job.

Metadata

A second key difference is the existence of metadata. The *Sedona Glossary*[3] defines metadata as "data typically stored electronically that describes characteristics of" electronically stored information (ESI) and explains that metadata "can describe how, when, and by whom ESI was collected, created, accessed, modified and how it is formatted." A pocket guide

archive copies of documents; for e-mail, that meant printing them or keeping them "on your hard drive").

[2] *See, e.g.*, Cache La Poudre Feeds, LLC v. Land O'Lakes, Inc., et al., 2007 U.S. Dist. LEXIS 15277 (D. Colo. Mar. 2, 2007) (wiping clean the computer hard drives of former employees, among other conduct, was sanctionable under the circumstances, but since the prejudice was not substantial, sanctions were limited to $5,000 and reimbursement of certain court-reporting costs).

[3] The Sedona Conference Glossary: E-Discovery & Digital Information Management 2nd Ed. (Dec. 2007), http://www.thesedonaconference.org/dlt.Form?did-TSCGlossary_12_07.pdf (*Sedona Glossary*). The *Sedona Glossary* continues by explaining that metadata can be "altered intentionally or inadvertently." It can be "extracted when native files are converted to image." Some metadata, such as file dates and sizes, "can easily be seen by users"; other metadata "can be hidden or embedded and unavailable to computer users who are not technically adept. Metadata is generally not reproduced in full form when a document is printed to paper or electronic image." The Sedona Conference working group series "is a series of think-tanks consisting of leading jurists, lawyers, experts and consultants brought together by a desire to address various 'tipping point' issues in each area under consideration." *See* http://www.thesedonaconference.org/. The Sedona Conference Working Group on Electronic Document Retention and Production has also published the second edition of Best Practices Recommendations & Principles for Addressing Electronic Document Production (June 2007). The document can be downloaded by going to the Sedona Conference website. *See* http://www.thesedonaconference.org/dltForm?did=TSC_PRINCP_2nd_ed_607.pdf.

provided to federal judges by the United States Judicial Conference gives this definition of metadata:

> Metadata, which most computer users never see, provide information about an electronic file, such as the date it was created, its author, when and by whom it was edited, what edits were made, and, in the case of e-mail, the history of its transmission.[4]

Yet another description appears in *Williams v. Sprint/United Mgmt. Co.*, 230 F.R.D. 640, 646 (D. Kan. 2005) (footnotes omitted):

> Some examples of metadata for electronic documents include: a file's name, a file's location (e.g., directory structure or pathname), file format or file type, file size, file dates (e.g., creation date, date of last data modification, date of last data access, and date of last metadata modification), and file permissions (e.g., who can read the data, who can write to it, who can run it). Some metadata, such as file dates and sizes, can easily be seen by users; other metadata can be hidden or embedded and unavailable to computer users who are not technically adept.[5]

Appendix I contains a good example of embarrassing metadata identified by a third party in a Microsoft Word document that the British government posted on June 30, 2003. The document was a dossier on Iraqi security and intelligence.[6]

Deleted Data That Do Not Die

A third key difference is that digital data can survive deletion, while discarded paper is not likely to be found again. The *Sedona Glossary* gives this definition of "deleted data":

> Deleted Data is data that existed on the computer as live data and which have been deleted by the computer system or end-user activity. Deleted data may remain on storage media in whole or in part

[4] Managing Discovery of Electronic Information: A Pocket Guide for Judges at 3 (2007), http://www.uscourts.gov/rules/eldscpkt.pdf.

[5] Examples of metadata that may be stored in Microsoft Word 2003 documents can be found at http://support.microsoft.com/kb/825576/ (e.g., your name, initials, company, or organization name; the name of your computer; the name of the network server or hard disk where you saved the document; other file properties and summary information; document revisions; document versions; template information; hidden text; and comments).

[6] Microsoft has since eliminated the software features that allowed the metadata in question to be discovered but the example serves as a good illustration of "metadata mining."

> until they are overwritten or "wiped." Even after the data itself has been wiped, directory entries, pointers or other information relating to the deleted data may remain on the computer. "Soft deletions" are data marked as deleted (and not generally available to the end-user after such marking), but not yet physically removed or overwritten. Soft-deleted data can be restored with complete integrity.

So, for example, a computer user moves data to "trash" or the "recycle bin." Until the trash or bin is emptied, the data remain fully restorable. Once the trash or bin is emptied, forensic experts may be able to reconstruct data fragments to recreate the deleted file, unless the storage media in question has been "wiped" (typically by software designed to achieve this aim).[7]

Multiple Sources of Data

A fourth key difference is the proliferation of data sources over paper. A "key player" in a particular dispute may have information stored in several places, and multiple copies of the same information may exist in multiple places. Consider these possibilities:

1. Office desktop storage media;
2. Office backup storage media;

---

[7] *See, e.g.,* Kucala Enterprises, Ltd. v. Auto Wax Co., Inc., 2003 U.S. Dist. LEXIS 8833 (N.D. Ill. 2003). In the course of this patent infringement case, Kucala installed and used software called "Evidence Eliminator" on a computer, just hours before it was to be examined by Auto Wax's computer specialist. The magistrate judge explained that "Evidence Eliminator" is a program designed to clean computer hard drives of data that may have been deleted by the user but still remain on the hard drive. Kucala also threw two other computers away during the litigation. He did so, he said, because they had crashed and were of no use to him. Kucala also admitted destroying documents, contrary to his attorney's advice, because he was afraid the defendant would not honor a protective order that was in place. Auto Wax's computer specialist inspected the computer on which Kucala had installed "Evidence Eliminator," and confirmed that the software had been used to delete and overwrite more than 14,000 files. Auto Wax filed a motion for sanctions alleging prejudice as a result of Kucala's destruction of one computer and deletion of relevant discovery from two others. Auto Wax sought a default judgment, attorneys' fees, expert fees, and costs. The magistrate judge found that Kucala had acted unreasonably, with gross negligence, and in flagrant disregard of the district court's order by deleting files just hours before Auto Wax's computer specialist was to inspect his computer. The magistrate judge recommended that the district court dismiss the action and require Kucala to pay the costs and attorneys' fees incurred by Auto Wax from the time Kucala deleted the files until the hearing.

3. Office laptop storage media;
4. Optical discs like CDs (compact disc) or DVDs (digital video disc or digital versatile disc);
5. Floppy disks;
6. Flash or "thumb" drives;
7. Home computer storage media, including external hard drives and portable drives;
8. Personal laptop storage media;
9. Office or home voice mail;
10. Cell phone voice mail;
11. Personal digital assistants (e.g., Blackberry);
12. Web-based storage;
13. Home or personal e-mail systems;
14. Devices that send or receive instant messages;
15. Printers, scanners, and copiers with computer memory;
16. Memory cards (e.g., from cameras); and
17. In appropriate cases, global positioning system devices.

Backup Tapes

Another key difference between the paper and electronic worlds is the existence of backup tapes,[8] which are typically used for disaster-recovery purposes. Backup tapes contain extraordinary amounts of information. To illustrate, consider this explanation from the United States Judicial Center's *Manual for Complex Litigation* of the volume of electronic information:

> The sheer volume of such data, when compared with conventional paper documentation, can be staggering. A floppy disk, with 1.44 megabytes, is the equivalent of 720 typewritten pages of plain text. A CD-ROM, with 650 megabytes, can hold up to 325,000 typewritten pages. One gigabyte is the equivalent of 500,000 typewritten pages. Large corporate computer networks create backup data measured

[8] The *Sedona Glossary* defines "backup tapes" as follows: "Magnetic tape used to store copies of ESI, for use when restoration or recovery of data is required. ESI on backup tape is generally recorded and stored sequentially, rather than randomly, meaning in order to locate and access a specific file or data set, all ESI on the tape preceding the target must first be read, a time-consuming and inefficient process. Backup tapes typically use data compression, which increases restoration time and expense, given the lack of uniform standards governing data compression."

> in terabytes, or 1,000,000 megabytes: each terabyte[9] represents the equivalent of 500 billion typewritten pages of plain text.

Manual for Complex Litigation (4th), § 11.446.[10]

One of the reasons backup tapes contain so much data is duplication. For example, after a thirty-day month, an entity that backs up daily, weekly, and monthly will have thirty daily tapes, four or five weekly tapes, and one monthly tape. The tapes will contain all the information stored at the time of the backup. Hence, a daily backup on a Tuesday will contain Monday and Tuesday's information. A weekly backup on Friday will contain whatever information that has been stored since the last weekly backup plus all the information contained on the prior weekly backup tape. The monthly tape will contain whatever has been stored since the prior month's backup tape and will duplicate much of the information on the daily and weekly backup tapes. Backup tapes are recycled after a period of time as well.

Typically, backup tapes are not reasonably accessible, as compared with "active data," which users can access easily.[11]

Perhaps as significant, backup tapes may be the only places certain documents reside. Unless they were printed, prior versions of a document may exist only on backup—they would be overwritten each time the user edits the file contained in active data storage. An individual that does not archive an e-mail on his or her individual hard drive will lose

---

[9] A "byte" is the basic measurement of "most computer data and consists of 8 bits." A "bit" is a "binary digit." A bit consists of either a 0 or 1. Generalizing, in computer code, for a word processing system, 0s and 1s (electronically switched off or on) are strung together to represent letters, numbers, and punctuation. There are 1,024 bytes in a "kilobyte," 1,048,576 bytes in a megabyte, 1,073,741,824 bytes in a gigabyte, and 1,099,511,627,776 bytes in a terabyte. *See* http://kb.iu.edu/data/ackw.html.

[10] Http://www.fjc.gov/public/home.nsf/autoframe?openform&url_l=/public/home.nsf/inavgeneral?openpage&url_r=/public/home.nsf/pages/470.

[11] One court has described the difference between data that are "accessible" and data that are "inaccessible." Data that are (1) "online" or archived on current computer systems (such as hard drives), (2) "near-line," such as that stored on optical discs or magnetic tape that is stored in a robotic storage library from which records can be retrieved in two minutes or less, or (3) "off-line" but in storage or archives, such as removable optical disc (e.g., CD-ROM or Digital Versatile Disc (DVD)) or magnetic tape media (e.g., Digital Linear Tape (DLT)), are readily accessible using standard search engines because the data are retained in machine readable format. Zubulake v. UBS Warburg LLC, 217 F.R.D. 309, 318-320 (S.D.N.Y. 2003). On the other hand, (1) routine disaster recovery backup tapes that save information in compressed, sequential, and nonindexed format, and (2) erased, fragmented, or damaged data, are generally inaccessible, because a time-consuming, expensive restoration process is required to obtain information. *Id.* at 319-320.

that e-mail to backup after a period of time. Hence, backup tapes may reveal whether an individual has deleted an e-mail.[12]

Retrieval of information from backup tapes can be costly. Costs can include separate charges for restoration, retrieval, and review. In *Zubulake v. UBS Warburg LLC,* 216 F.R.D. 280 (S.D.N.Y. 2003),[13] for example, there was a battle over the production of seventy-seven backup tapes. The district court ordered UBS Warburg to restore—at its expense—five tapes to give the district court an idea of the cost to restore and the relevance of the information contained on the backup tapes. The cost to restore five backup tapes was $19,003.43, and it resulted in the production of six hundred e-mails responsive to the plaintiff's request for production. UBS Warburg estimated that the cost to restore the remaining seventy-two tapes was $273,649.39, and that the cost to review the data before production would be $107,694.72.

One of the many reasons that review costs can be so high is that it is not easy to determine which backup data is protected by the attorney-client privilege. Privileged communications involving in-house counsel and outside-counsel's privileged communications with a client can be buried among millions of pages of documents on a backup tape. To identify privileged documents is both time-consuming and costly.

---

[12] Backup tapes will not capture an e-mail received by an individual and deleted the same day. To illustrate, in Zubulake v. UBS Warburg LLC, 217 F.R.D. 309 (S.D.N.Y. 2003), the district court explained UBS Warburg's electronic storage architecture: "UBS backed up its e-mails at three intervals: (1) daily, at the end of each day, (2) weekly, on Friday nights, and (3) monthly, on the last business day of the month. Nightly backup tapes were kept for twenty working days, weekly tapes for one year, and monthly tapes for three years. After the relevant time period elapsed, the tapes were recycled." *Id.* at 314. The district court explained why backup tapes might not contain certain e-mails: "Of course, periodic backups such as UBS's necessarily entails the loss of certain e-mails. Because backups were conducted only intermittently, some e-mails that were deleted from the server were never backed up. For example, if a user both received and deleted an e-mail on the same day, it would not reside on any backup tape. Similarly, an e-mail received and deleted within the span of one month would not exist on the monthly backup, although it might exist on a weekly or daily backup, if those tapes still exist." *Id.* at 314, n.25.

[13] Ms. Zubulake alleged she was a victim of gender discrimination and was eventually terminated. She then filed an additional claim that she was retaliated against for complaining about the employment practices of her supervisor. 216 F.R.D. at 281. The district court explained that under the Federal Rules of Civil Procedure, the presumption is that the producing party pays for production of accessible data. In addition, the district court held that the cost to review should always be borne by the producing party. With respect to the cost to retrieve, the district court evaluated each of seven factors identified by the district court as relevant to the determination of who should pay this cost, and decided to shift 25 percent of the cost to the requesting party, Ms. Zubulake. 216 F.R.D. at 283-90.

Key Players

In the paper world, there is not necessarily a premium placed on correctly identifying so-called key players—the people with knowledge or information about a claim—because many companies keep paper for a long time. In the electronic world, it is much more significant to identify the correct key players because any delay in doing so can result in the loss of relevant information.

For example, in *Consolidated Aluminum Co. v. Alcoa*, 2006 U.S. Dist. LEXIS 66642 (E.D. La. July 19, 2006), four key players initially were identified in November 2002 when Alcoa sent a demand letter to Conalco for costs associated with an environmental cleanup. Later, in 2003, Conalco decided to sue, seeking a declaration of nonliability. In 2005, Conalco issued a request for production that prompted Alcoa to identify eleven more key players. In the interim, however, the e-mails of these eleven individuals had been erased because of Alcoa's e-mail backup retention protocol.[14] Conalco moved for sanctions. The district court refused to grant punitive sanctions, but required Alcoa to pay the reasonable costs and fees Conalco incurred to bring the motion for sanctions, and also to pay the cost of redeposing up to thirteen people. The court also allowed Conalco to serve certain additional discovery requests.

Similarly, in *E*Trade Securities LLC v. Deutsche Bank AG*, 2005 U.S. Dist. LEXIS 3021 (D. Minn. Feb. 17, 2005), in 2001, defendant NSI put a litigation hold on backup tapes, but not on e-mail messages. The reason was that NSI had a practice of backing up all e-mail messages. However, NSI also recycled its backup tapes after three years, a policy that the company did not change even though the litigation continued more than three years beyond the date of the litigation hold. When it became clear in 2004 that additional e-mail boxes needed to be searched beyond those of the initial key players, the e-mails were no longer available. As a sanction, the court approved an adverse inference instruction.

---

[14] Alcoa submitted an affidavit describing the protocol: "Once every week, all messages older than thirty (30) days in a user's Exchange mailbox are moved to a 'System Cleanup' folder. At the same time, all messages older than fifteen (15) days (forty-five (45) days total) in a user's System Cleanup folder are deleted and are no longer directly recoverable by the user . . . . In addition, Alcoa's disaster recovery system retains email for the trailing six (6) months." 2006 U.S. Dist. LEXIS at *19, n.12. That prompted the magistrate judge to say: "Thus, it is possible that relevant emails for the six (6) months prior to November 2002 could have been retrieved, had Alcoa properly suspended its routine document destruction policy when it became aware of potential litigation with Consolidated in November 2002." *Id.* at *19.

Forms of Production

In the world of electronically stored information, parties have choices about the form of production. A requesting party may seek production in "native" format, which refers to the file as it exists on the other party's storage media, together with associated metadata. A producing party may prefer to produce documents in "tagged image file format" (TIFF)[15] or "portable document format" (PDF)[16] in order to, among other things, bates-label the documents. Vendors should be able to link meaningful metadata to an associated TIFF or PDF image depending on the parties' agreement or the scope of a court's order on production of electronically stored information.[17] Of course, there is always paper as well. Electronic files might be printed for production in paper format.

---

[15] The *Sedona Glossary* defines TIFF as: "A widely used and supported graphic file formats [sic] for storing bit-mapped images, with many different compression formats and resolutions. File name has .TIF extension. Can be black and white, gray-scaled, or color. Images are stored in tagged fields, and programs use the tags to accept or ignore fields, depending on the application."

[16] The *Sedona Glossary* defines PDF as: "An imaging file format technology developed by Adobe Systems. PDF captures formatting information from a variety of applications in such a way that they can be viewed and printed as they were intended in their original application by practically any computer, on multiple platforms, regardless of the specific application in which the original was created. PDF files may be text-searchable or image-only. Adobe® Reader, a free application distributed by Adobe Systems, is required to view a file in PDF format. Adobe® Acrobat, an application marketed by Adobe Systems, is required to edit, capture text, or otherwise manipulate a file in PDF format."

[17] According to the *Sedona Glossary* definition of "native format," "static" formats such as TIFF or PDF, "are designed to retain an image of the document as it would look viewed in the original creating application but do not allow metadata to be viewed or the document information to be manipulated." *Cf.* White v. The Graceland College Center et al., 2008 U.S. Dist. LEXIS 63088 (D. Kan. Aug. 7, 2008). In this matter, the magistrate ordered the producing party to produce emails and their attachments in native format after they had been produced in paper form. The requesting party had not specified a form of production thereby triggering Rule 34(b)(2)(E)(ii) which provides that, in such a case, the producing party has the option to produce in a form or forms in which the information is "ordinarily maintained or in a reasonably usable form or forms." Reduced to its essence, however, the magistrate's ruling was premised on the importance that metadata played in the requesting party's case. To get to this result, the magistrate said that the producing party should have produced the electronic information in native format since that was "a reasonably usable form" and—because of the need for the metadata—paper was not such a form on the facts of this case. *Cf.* Williams v. Sprint/United Management Co., 2006 WL 3691604, *14 (D. Kan. Dec. 12, 2006), where the same magistrate judge refused to require production in native format because no need for metadata was shown.

Parties wishing to perform electronic searches will want data in a searchable format. In addition, there may be reasons to obtain electronically stored information in different formats. For example, word-processing documents could be imaged with word-search capabilities while spreadsheets may be produced in native format to view the formulae used in the spreadsheet.

Vendor Contracts

Because of the different forms of production for different forms of data, one can readily see that in major productions of electronically stored information, litigation counsel will need help.[18] There is no shortage of firms willing to provide e-discovery assistance. Contracts with these firms must take into account a number of issues, including the following:

- What data will be collected from what locations or types of storage media?
- How will the collected data be transferred to the vendor and will it need to be encrypted or sent via other secured method?
- How will the data be extracted, and what steps will be taken to address—for example—file integrity, de-duplication of data, maintenance of attachments with e-mails, proper separation of documents, preservation of metadata, extraction of embedded information, processing of foreign language documents, identification or labeling of documents, and chain of custody?
- Are there any issues with collecting, transferring, or processing documents from a country subject to data protection, privacy, or blocking laws?
- Where and how will the data be stored and, if hosted by the vendor, at what price?
- What encryption, virus protection, or other security measures will be taken to protect the stored data?[19]
- How will the data be accessed by the client?
- Will any storage media have to be imaged?

[18] Corporate lawyers setting up large data banks for a deal may also need help.

[19] *See* New Jersey Ethics Opinion 701 (2006) (lawyer must take reasonable care to protect the confidentiality of electronic files and where the lawyer has entrusted the files to an outside provider, there must be "an enforceable obligation to preserve confidentiality and security," and "available technology to guard against reasonably foreseeable attempts to infiltrate the data" must be used.) http://www.judiciary.state.nj.us/notices/ethics/ACPE_Opinion701_ElectronicStorage_12022005.pdf.

- Will forensic examination of any storage media have to be undertaken?
- What search and filter tools will be utilized, are there any additional charges for their use, and who will make this decision?
- How and at what cost will information be reviewed and processed if the vendor is unable to do so using its normal processes?[20]
- In what form will the data be produced to a requesting party and who will do the quality control check on the production?
- How will production be tracked and will the tracking account for special productions or production in various formats?
- If the form of production changes, will contract costs be affected? If so, under what circumstances?
- What is the pricing structure? Fixed fee? Price per gigabyte? Variable rates for various tasks?
- Are there any special costs for processing computer images or backup tapes, or for any other activities?
- Under what circumstances will change orders on price be permissible, if at all?
- If there are problems with data extraction or data production, who bears responsibility for any additional costs associated with the resolution of those problems?
- Who bears the risk of software failure, file corruption, storage media deterioration, and hardware failure or replacement?
- If sanctions are awarded because of the failure of a vendor to exercise the appropriate degree of care, who pays the sanctions?
- Will you include a confidentiality term? Assuming so, what should it say? How will confidential data be treated in the event of litigation with the vendor?
- Will a limitation-of-liability clause be permitted? If so, at what limit?
- Should there be an indemnity provision and who should it favor?

---

[20] My colleague and friend, Arlen Tanner, Esq., is an extraordinarily talented member of Shook, Hardy & Bacon's E-Discovery Working Group with rich, technical experience. He reports that there may be files that a vendor cannot open because of the vendor's software. When there are resistant-to-processing documents like this, they may be viewable using alternative software and can then be imaged, reviewed, and included in the production if responsive. Vendors may not be motivated to process these files because they require individual attention and the identification of viewing software. Personal Communication with Arlen Tanner, Esq. (April 21, 2008).

- Will insurance play a role in allocating risk under the contract?
- What will the contract say about termination?
- Is the client in a position to receive the data immediately in the event the contract is terminated?
- Are there "data-return" charges in the event of termination? What data will be returned, at what cost, if any, and in what format?[21]
- Should there be dispute resolution mechanisms built into the contract? If so, which ones?
- What law should govern?
- Should there be a venue clause in the event of judicial dispute resolution?
- Should there be a waiver of jury trial?
- Should attorneys' fees be recoverable by a prevailing party if a dispute requires judicial or arbitral resolution?

Not every e-discovery obligation will require a vendor contract, but many e-discovery obligations will require a vendor. As a result, one or more of these questions may still apply.

[21] The data might be returned in a manner that requires a new vendor to reprocess it. Sometimes review, redaction, de-duplication, and production data are lost. Or information is stored by the vendor in a proprietary format or costs a significant amount to recover or is not defined as the client's "data" for data-return purposes. Personal Communication with Arlen Tanner, Esq. (April 21, 2008).

CHAPTER TWO

A Primer on the Federal E-Discovery Rules

Let me next briefly discuss the December 1, 2006, amendments to the Federal Rules of Civil Procedure as they relate to e-discovery. Fed. R. Civ. P. 26(f) requires that counsel confer shortly after a lawsuit is filed to map out a discovery plan and otherwise agree on a pretrial schedule that the district court can consider at the conference required under Fed. R. Civ. P. 16. Also, under Fed. R. Civ. P. 26(f) counsel must also discuss: (1) "any issues"[1] relating to "disclosure" of electronically stored information, "including the form or forms in which it should be produced,"[2] and

---

[1] *See* Mancia v Mayflower Textile Servs. Co., (D. Md. Oct. 15, 2008). In this matter, the magistrate discusses the role that cooperation must play for the discovery system to work: "Rule 26(g) charges that those responsible for the success or failure of pretrial discovery—the trial judge and the lawyers for the adverse parties—with approaching the process properly: discovery must be initiated and responded to responsibly, in accordance with the letter and spirit of the discovery rules, to achieve a proper purpose (i.e., not to harass, unnecessarily delay, or impose needless expense), and be proportional to what is at issue in the litigation, and if it is not, the judge is expected to impose appropriate sanctions to punish and deter . . . . However central the adversary system is to our way of formal dispute resolution, there is nothing inherent in it that precludes cooperation between the parties and their attorneys during the litigation process to achieve orderly and cost effective discovery of the competing facts on which the system depends."

[2] A lack of communication or miscommunication by counsel is a common cause of e-discovery controversy among parties. The requirement that lawyers discuss e-discovery issues up front should minimize the potential for later disputes. Lawyers who fail to comprehend a client's electronic information system over the period of time relevant to the

(2) any issues relating to claims of privilege, including assertion of privilege after production. Fed. R. Civ. P. 16(b)(3) then provides that the district court's scheduling order may: "(iii) provide for disclosure or discovery of electronically stored information," and "(iv) include any agreements the parties reach for asserting claims of privilege or of protection as trial-preparation material after information is produced."

Fed. R. Civ. P. 26(b)(2)(B) distinguishes between "accessible" and "inaccessible" documents:

> A party need not provide discovery of electronically stored information from sources that the party identifies as not reasonably accessible because of undue burden or cost.[3] On motion to compel discovery or for a protective order, the party from whom discovery is sought must show that the information is not reasonably accessible because of undue burden or cost. If that showing is made, the court may nonetheless order discovery from such sources if the requesting party shows good cause, considering the limitations of Rule 26(b)(2)(C). The court may specify conditions for such discovery.[4]

---

claims in question are treading in perilous waters. *See, e.g.*, Evolution, Inc. v. The Suntrust Bank, et al., 2004 U.S. Dist. LEXIS 20490 (D. Ks. 2004), where a special master had to be appointed to straighten out the parties' e-discovery disputes, generating a bill of $52,140, which was allocated 70 percent to the defendant, in part, because of defendant's lack of digital cooperation.

[3] Note that the producing party must "identify" the sources of electronically stored information that are inaccessible because of "undue burden or cost." Even if costs are not "undue," the burden of searching some kinds of information may be. An "undue burden," of course, is whatever a judge decides it is. What is certain is that counsel must comprehend a client's inaccessible sources of information early and thoroughly to be in the best position to educate a judge who will decide what is "undue." The Civil Rules Advisory Committee's Report gives examples of sources of electronically stored information that may qualify under this standard: backup tapes intended for disaster recovery purposes "that are often not indexed, organized, or susceptible to electronic searching"; "legacy data" from "obsolete systems and is unintelligible on the successor systems"; data that was deleted "but remains in fragmented form, requiring a modern version of forensics to restore and retrieve"; and "databases that were designed to create certain information in certain ways and that cannot readily create very different kinds or forms of information." Report of the Civil Rules Advisory Committee (May 27, 2005 (as revised July 25, 2005)), p. 40 (hereafter 2005 Adv. Comm. Report, p. __). The Advisory Committee Report can be found at Appendix C to the "Summary of the Report of the Judicial Conference Committee on Rules of Practice and Procedure" (Sept. 2005), which can be found at http://www.uscourts.gov/rules/Reports/ST09-2005.pdf.

[4] Litigants can expect courts to develop balancing tests to determine when a burden "tilts" in favor of the requesting party (e.g., because there is a strong likelihood that material in-

Fed. R. Civ. P. 26(b)(5)(B) addresses what a party who inadvertently produced privileged documents must now do (give notice and preserve the information until the claim is resolved) and what the receiving party must do (among other things, promptly return, sequester, or destroy the information and any copies, and not use or disclose the information).

Fed. R. Civ. P. 33(d) discusses the option to produce business records in lieu of answering an interrogatory, where the answer to the interrogatory may be derived or ascertained from business records, and the burden of deriving or ascertaining the answer is substantially the same for the party serving the interrogatory as for the party served. Fed. R. Civ. P. 33(d) now defines business records as "including electronically stored information." Access to hardware, software, technical support, passwords, source code, or other assistance may have to be provided by the responding party, limiting perhaps the utility of this change.

Fed. R. Civ. P. 34(a)(1)(A) now distinguishes between "documents" and "electronically stored information." It provides that a party may serve a request to any other party to produce "any designated documents or electronically stored information." As a means to control and estimate costs, and to evaluate the likelihood that electronic storage media contain relevant information, Fed. R. Civ. P. 34(a)(1) incorporates a "sampling" technique already employed by a number of courts. *See, e.g., Medtronic Sofamor Danek, Inc. v. Sofamor Danek Holdings, Inc.*, 2003 U.S. Dist. LEXIS 8587 (W.D. Tenn. May 13, 2003). The producing party can now be asked to permit the requesting party "to test, or sample any designated documents or electronically stored information—including sound recordings, images, and other data or data compilations stored in any medium—from which information can be obtained, translated, if necessary, by respondent into reasonably usable form."

Under Fed. R. Civ. P. 34(b)(1)(C), a requesting party may specify a form of production, subject to objection by the producing party. Under Fed. R. Civ. P. 34(b)(2)(D) and (E), if no form is specified by the request-

formation is located only on the inaccessible storage media) or the producing party (e.g., if the overbreadth of the request for information is blatant), and to use cost-shifting to level the playing field. *Cf. In re:* Priceline.com Inc., 2005 U.S. Dist. LEXIS 33636, *11 (D. Conn. Dec. 8, 2005) (where the district court set forth nine directives to manage e-discovery including one requiring restoration of 223 backup tapes—estimated to cost $200 to $800 per tape in addition to the cost of searching the files, culling for duplicate files, and converting responsive files for production. The court said discovery "shall proceed on a measured basis, with cost-shifting determinations made at each step of the process.")

ing party, the producing party can produce electronically stored information in the form in which it is ordinarily maintained or in a form that is reasonably usable. A producing party need only produce electronically stored information in one form. If objection is made to the requested form of production and agreement is not reached on the form of production, the district court must resolve the dispute and will almost certainly be guided by an evaluation of costs and benefits.

Fed. R. Civ. P. 45 addressing subpoenas has been conformed to new Rules 26 and 34.

Fed. R. Civ. P. 37(e) addresses sanctions for the loss of electronic information. It provides:

> Absent exceptional circumstances, a court may not impose sanctions under these rules on a party for failing to provide electronically stored information lost as a result of the routine, good-faith operation of an electronic information system.[5]

Against this backdrop, let's now explore the ethics of e-discovery.

[5] "Exceptional circumstances" are not defined, but a violation of a preservation order—perhaps even an internal litigation hold—would presumably satisfy this standard. The sanctions referenced are those "under these rules." Courts, of course, have "inherent power" to issue sanctions irrespective of the rules, so this power is unaffected by new Fed. R. Civ. P. 37(e). The language, "routine, good-faith operation of an electronic information system" cannot be read in isolation. Every litigant has a duty to preserve relevant documents and electronically stored information, and that duty can arise long before a complaint is filed. In a post-complaint setting, the loss of information—e.g., the automatic deletion of certain employees' e-mail—can easily be routine if no changes are made in a litigant's electronic information system to control the loss. It may not be in "good faith" if the duty to preserve had already attached to those employees' e-mail.

CHAPTER THREE

E-Discovery Under the Model Rules

A number of Model Rules may apply in an e-discovery context.[1]

Competence Under Model Rule 1.1 and the Rise of E-Discovery Counsel

Model Rule 1.1 provides:

> A lawyer shall provide competent representation to a client. Competent representation requires the legal knowledge, skill, thoroughness and preparation reasonably necessary for the representation.

Comment [6] adds:

> To maintain the requisite knowledge and skill, a lawyer should keep abreast of changes in the law and its practice, engage in continuing study and education and comply with all continuing legal education requirements to which the lawyer is subject.

After having read the brief tutorial above, are you competent to handle e-discovery? You may know how to copy 250 responsive word-processing documents onto a rewritable CD. You may not know that if you review documents on a rewritable CD before you transmit it, you may change the metadata associated with the documents you

[1] While the discussion that follows may appear to be exhaustive, I have selected certain rules for coverage and do not represent that I have identified every Model Rule that may apply to a particular ethics question involving e-discovery.

reviewed.[2] You may know what it means to secure a hard drive for forensic imaging. You may not know that merely turning on the computer associated with the drive will cause changes in the drive. It is one thing to handle a production of e-mail from a couple of key players. It is quite another to manage the production of e-mail, spreadsheets, presentation files, database information, and word processing documents from different software and storage systems, in multiple locations in the United States or perhaps throughout the world, where numerous key players may have different storage habits and some locations may have different retention policies than other locations, and where translation issues may become significant. A lawyer should know when to tell a client to preserve documents, but will the lawyer know enough to identify when the duty to preserve attaches and whether backup processes should be suspended until the client and the lawyer can understand whether there might be a duty to preserve electronic information stored on backup tapes?

E-discovery will change litigation as many litigators have known it because they are not independently competent to handle production of electronic documents. They also may need assistance negotiating with a vendor regarding the proper scope of an electronic production. Technology has increased productivity in our personal and business lives. Yet because technology allows parties to store so much information so cheaply, it has the potential to greatly increase the cost of litigation if lawyers are not competent to handle e-discovery smartly and sensibly, whatever the amount in controversy.

Comment [1] to Model Rule 1.1 identifies relevant factors in determining whether a lawyer has the requisite knowledge and skill to handle a particular matter. They include,

> the relative complexity and specialized nature of the matter, the lawyer's general experience, the lawyer's training and experience in the field in question, the preparation and study the lawyer is able to give the matter and whether it is feasible to refer the matter to, or associate or consult with, a lawyer of established competence in the field in question.

---

[2] If the CD is not rewritable (i.e., it is "read only" or "CD-R"), a review will not affect the metadata associated with the documents on the disc. However, depending upon how one copies the documents from a CD-R to other media or even to create a new CD-R, all of the metadata may not stay the same. Opening files from a thumb drive or a hard drive will alter the metadata associated with the files. Personal Communication with Arlen Tanner, Esq. (April 21, 2008).

For entities facing numerous lawsuits, it is not at all unusual any longer to have "e-discovery counsel" who (1) have become familiar with the architecture of the client's electronically stored information; (2) can meaningfully explain that architecture, especially with respect to accessible information and information that is not reasonably accessible because of undue burden or cost; (3) understand the cost implications of each e-discovery commitment; (4) will maintain consistency in e-discovery "meet-and-confer" sessions in different jurisdictions; and (5) can direct an efficient and properly defensible collection and preservation effort. Where such counsel do not exist, lawyers must be able to take these factors, among others, into account to satisfy the requirements of Rule 1.1.[3]

If the lawyer or the lawyer's colleagues do not have the e-discovery expertise, and e-discovery counsel is not involved, finding a vendor who spends the client's money wisely, and whose mission is to work itself out of a job might be the lawyer's best friend to satisfy the requirements of Model Rule 1.1.[4]

Rule 4.4 and Ethics Issues Associated with Inadvertent Production of Privileged Information

E-discovery increases the potential for inadvertent production of privileged information. Producing parties typically do not have mechanisms in place to retrieve, restore, and cost-effectively identify electronically stored information that is privileged. Hence, individual documents have to be reviewed for privilege determinations. In a production of hundreds of thousands, or millions, of pages of electronic documents, a privileged document or two might be missed. Does a lawyer who inadvertently

---

[3] Comment [5] to Model Rule 1.1 adds that handling a matter competently "includes inquiry into and analysis of the factual and legal elements of the problem, and use of methods and procedures meeting the standards of competent practitioners. It also includes adequate preparation. The required attention and preparation are determined in part by what is at stake; major litigation and complex transactions ordinarily require more extensive treatment than matters of lesser complexity and consequence. An agreement between the lawyer and the client regarding the scope of the representation may limit the matters for which the lawyer is responsible. *See* Rule 1.2(c)." Rule 1.2(c) provides: "A lawyer may limit the scope of the representation if the limitation is reasonable under the circumstances and the client gives informed consent."

[4] Attending appropriate training programs may also be necessary. *See* Florida Ethics Op. 06-2, discussed below (citing to its comment identical to Comment [6] of Model Rule 1.1, Florida Rule of Professional Conduct 4-1.1 "may necessitate a lawyer's continuing training and education in the use of technology in transmitting and receiving electronic information in order to protect client information under Rule 1.6(a)").

receives a privileged document have an ethical obligation to notify the sender? Or suppose the lawyer is the sender who later discovers the inadvertent transmittal of a privileged document to a requesting party. What should the lawyer do?

Model Rule 4.4(b) and Fed. R. Civ. P. 26(b)(5)(b) now address this subject. Model Rule 4.4 provides that a lawyer who receives documents that the lawyer knows or reasonably should know were sent inadvertently[5] must "promptly notify the sender." Rule 4.4(b) reads in full:

> (b) A lawyer who receives a document relating to the representation of the lawyer's client[6] and knows or reasonably should know that the document was inadvertently sent shall promptly[7] notify the sender.

Comment [2] to Rule 4.4 suggests that Rule 4.4 is not limited to privileged documents, but embraces any documents "that were mistakenly sent or produced by opposing parties or their lawyers." Comment [2] further states that whether the lawyer is required to do more than give notice to the sender, "such as returning the original document, is a matter of law beyond the scope of these Rules, as is the question of whether the privileged status of a document has been waived."[8]

---

[5] How is a lawyer to know whether a privileged document was sent inadvertently? In some cases, it will be obvious by the first line or few lines of the document. Or one might just ask one's opponent.

[6] The phrase, "relating to the representation of the client," is language taken from Rule 1.6, which is discussed below. A document or information "relating to the representation of a client" includes one covered by the attorney-client privilege.

[7] "Promptly" connotes an ethically required immediacy. While not every state has adopted Rule 4.4, it would still seem prudent for a lawyer-recipient, in the absence of an agreement between counsel or a court order, to advise everyone on the document review team that if a produced document appears to be privileged, it should be brought to the attention of the lawyer to ensure that the lawyer can determine whether the lawyer has a Rule 4.4 notification obligation.

[8] Comment [3] to Model Rule 4.4 provides: "Some lawyers may choose to return a document unread, for example, when the lawyer learns before receiving the document that it was inadvertently sent to the wrong address. Where a lawyer is not required by applicable law to do so, the decision to voluntarily return such a document is a matter of professional judgment ordinarily reserved to the lawyer. *See* Rules 1.2 and 1.4." Lawyers should consider "applicable law" and the RPC and ethics decisions of the jurisdiction in which the lawyer is offering legal services in evaluating how to proceed under Rule 4.4. Model Rule 1.2 provides in pertinent part that "a lawyer shall abide by a client's decisions concerning the objectives of representation and, as required by Rule 1.4, shall consult with the client as to the means by which they are to be pursued. A lawyer may take such action on behalf of the client as is impliedly authorized to carry out the representation." Model Rule 1.4(a)

Fed. R. Civ. P. 26(b)(5)(B) addresses the former question. It explains what a lawyer is supposed to do when informed by a sender that a privileged document was inadvertently transmitted. The lawyer does not have to notify the sender under Model Rule 4.4, because the sender discovered the mistake before the recipient did. Since December, 1, 2006, in federal courts, Fed. R. Civ. P. 26(b)(5)(B) provides:

> (B) If information produced in discovery is subject to a claim of privilege or of protection as trial preparation material, the party making the claim may notify any party that received the information of the claim and the basis for it. After being notified, a party must promptly return, sequester, or destroy the specified information and any copies it has; must not use or disclose the information until the claim is resolved; must take reasonable steps to retrieve the information if the party disclosed it before being notified; and may promptly present the information to the court under seal for a determination of the claim. The producing party must preserve the information until the claim is resolved.

In other words, returning the document(s) would not be required unless the recipient fails to sequester or destroy the documents. Regardless of the document-handling option chosen, the recipient must not use the information until the claim of privilege is resolved and must take reasonable steps to get copies of the documents back if they had already been disseminated before notice was received.

The combination of Rule 4.4 and Fed. R. Civ. P. 26(b)(5)(B) has sparked a debate among a number of ethics opinion writers on the propriety of mining metadata associated with the inadvertent transmittal or production of privileged documents.

ABA Formal Opinion 06-442: Mining of Metadata Permissible

In its Formal Opinion 06-442, the ABA Standing Committee on Ethics and Professional Responsibility[9] determined that the Model Rules

provides in part that a lawyer shall "(2) reasonably consult with the client about the means by which the client's objectives are to be accomplished;" "(3) keep the client reasonably informed about the status of the matter;" and "(5) consult with the client about any relevant limitation on the lawyer's conduct when the lawyer knows that the client expects assistance not permitted by the Rules of Professional Conduct or other law."

[9] The committee explained that its determination was based on the Model Rules and that, "The laws, court rules, regulations, rules of professional conduct and opinions promulgated in the individual jurisdictions are controlling." ABA Comm. on Ethics and Prof'l Responsibility, Formal Op. 06-442, n.2.

"generally"[10] permit a lawyer to "review and use embedded information contained in email and other electronic documents, whether received from opposing counsel, an adverse party or an agent of an adverse party." After first noting that most metadata is insignificant, the Standing Committee determined that the Model Rules "do not contain any specific prohibition against" the practice. Appearing to distinguish between the document and its associated metadata, the Standing Committee found Model Rule 4.4(b) inapplicable because it is silent "as to the ethical propriety of a lawyer's review or use of" metadata or an inadvertently produced privileged document.[11]

Florida Bar Ethics Committee Opinion 06-2: Mining of Metadata Impermissible

Under ABA Formal Opinion 06-442, a lawyer's compliance with Model Rule 4.4(b) is limited to notice to the sender. It does not include forbearance from reviewing privileged documents and any associated metadata. The Florida Bar Ethics Committee reached just the opposite conclusion in its Opinion 06-2 (September 15, 2006).[12] Relying on Florida Rule 4-4(b), which is identical to Model Rule 4.4(b), the Florida committee determined that it is the "recipient lawyer's" obligation,

> upon receiving an electronic communication or document from another lawyer, not to try to obtain from metadata information relating to the representation of the sender's client that the recipient knows or should know is not intended for the recipient. Any such metadata is to be considered by the receiving lawyer as confidential information which the sending lawyer did not intend to transmit. See, Ethics Opinion 93-3[13] and Rule 4-4.4(b), Florida Rules of Professional Conduct, effective May 22, 2006.

---

[10] Why the committee uses this word is not clear. Formal Opinion 06-442 does not offer a scenario under which a lawyer would be violating a Model Rule by reviewing metadata associated with a document received by the lawyer from an opposing counsel.

[11] If the document in question was produced in federal court litigation, Fed. R. Civ. P. 26(b)(5)(B) would undermine this rationale. It provides that once a recipient is on notice of an inadvertently produced piece of information that is privileged, the recipient must not "use or disclose" the "information until the claim of privilege is resolved." It is not likely that a federal district court would regard metadata associated with a privileged document as distinct from the document, if that is, in fact, part of the rationale underlying Formal Opinion 06-442.

[12] Http://www.floridabar.org/tfb/tfbetopin.nsf/SearchView/ETHICS,+OPINION+06-2?opendocument.

[13] Opinion 93-3 was issued by the Florida Bar Ethics Committee on February 1, 1994, and foreshadowed the outcome in Opinion 06-2. The problem addressed was "the inadvertent

Relying on Florida Rule 4-4(b), the committee added: "If the recipient lawyer inadvertently obtains information from metadata that the recipient knows or should know was not intended for the recipient, the lawyer must 'promptly notify the sender.'"

Maryland Bar Committee on Ethics 2007-09: Mining of Metadata Permissible

The Maryland State Bar Association Committee on Ethics, without citing ABA Formal Opinion 06-442, reached the same result as the ABA Standing Committee. In Ethics Docket 2007-09, the Maryland committee determined:[14]

> There is no ethical violation if the recipient attorney (or those working under the attorney's direction) reviews or makes use of the metadata without first ascertaining whether the sender intended to include such metadata.

The committee explained that because Maryland had not adopted Model Rule 4.4(b),[15] if there is no duty to notify the sender, there is no duty to

receipt or disclosure of attorney-client or work product privileged documents from an adversary. Such an inadvertent disclosure might occur as part of a document production, a misdirected facsimile or electronic mail transmission, a 'switched envelope' mailing, or misunderstood distribution list instructions." The committee determined that "an attorney, upon realizing or reasonably believing that he or she has received a document or documents that were inadvertently misdelivered, is ethically obligated to promptly notify the sender of the attorney's receipt of the documents. It is then up to the sender to take any further action." *See* https://www.floridabar.org/TFB/TFBETOpin.nsf/ca2dcdaa853ef7b885256728004f87db/0dce1fb368b9d50e85256b2f006ca7ce?OpenDocument. In the era of multijurisdictional practice, lawyers must be aware of state rules and state ethics opinions.

[14] *See* http://www.lexisnexis.com/applieddiscovery/LawLibrary/CourtRulesArticles/MarylandEOonMetadata.pdf.

[15] Maryland's RPC 4.4(b) provides: "In communicating with third persons, a lawyer representing a client in a matter shall not seek information relating to the matter that the lawyer knows or reasonably should know is protected from disclosure by statute or by an established evidentiary privilege, unless the protection has been waived. The lawyer who receives information that is protected from disclosure shall (1) terminate the communication immediately and (2) give notice of the disclosure to any tribunal in which the matter is pending and to the person entitled to enforce the protection against disclosure." Maryland's RPC 4.4(b) focuses on receipt of "information that is protected from disclosure" from "third persons" whereas Model Rule 4.4(b) focuses on receipt of "documents relating to the representation of the lawyer's client" where the recipient knows "or should know" that the documents were inadvertently sent.

refrain from review of the privileged documents inadvertently sent by the sender.[16]

D.C. Legal Ethics Committee Opinion 341: Mining of Metadata May Be Permissible

While Maryland has not adopted Model Rule 4.4(b), the District of Columbia Legal Ethics Committee, as explained in its September 2007 Opinion 341,[17] adopted a "more expansive" version of Rule 4.4(b) that has resulted in yet another variation of the proper ethical response of a lawyer who receives inadvertently produced privileged information. The D.C. committee also distinguished between review in nonlitigation and litigation settings.

D.C. Rule 4.4(b)[18] provides:

> A lawyer who receives a writing relating to the representation of a client and knows, before examining the writing, that it has been inadvertently sent, shall not examine the writing, but shall notify the sending party and abide by the instructions of the sending party regarding the return or destruction of the writing.

In other words, where the District of Columbia's rules of professional conduct govern, if a lawyer in a nonlitigation setting does not know that a

[16] The committee added that the lawyer-recipient "can, and probably should" communicate with the lawyer's client "concerning the pros and cons of whether to notify the sending attorney and/or to take such other action" that the lawyer believes is "appropriate." The committee did not explain its use of the qualifying word, "probably." Nor did it explain what other actions might be "appropriate." It did cite to Maryland RPC 1.4 and an accompanying footnote to Comment [3] to Model Rule 4.4 that, as noted earlier, provides that where an attorney is not required by applicable law to return an inadvertently produced document, "the decision to voluntarily return such a document is a matter of professional judgment ordinarily reserved to the lawyer. *See* Model Rules 1.2 and 1.4." As a reminder, Model Rule 1.2 provides in pertinent part that "a lawyer shall abide by a client's decisions concerning the objectives of representation and, as required by Rule 1.4, shall consult with the client as to the means by which they are to be pursued. A lawyer may take such action on behalf of the client as is impliedly authorized to carry out the representation." Model Rule 1.4(a) provides in part that that a lawyer shall "(2) reasonably consult with the client about the means by which the client's objectives are to be accomplished;" "(3) keep the client reasonably informed about the status of the matter"; and "(5) consult with the client about any relevant limitation on the lawyer's conduct when the lawyer knows that the client expects assistance not permitted by the Rules of Professional Conduct or other law." Maryland's version of Rule 1.4 includes subparagraph (3) and (5) quoted above, but not subparagraph (2).

[17] Http://www.dcbar.org/for_lawyers/ethics/legal_ethics/opinions/opinion341.cfm.

[18] *See* http://www.dcbar.org/new_rules/rules.cfm.

privileged document was inadvertently sent, the lawyer may review the document and any associated metadata with no apparent duty to notify the sender. Comment [3] to D.C. Rule 4.4(b) confirms this explanation:

> On the other hand, where writings containing client secrets or confidences are inadvertently delivered to an adversary lawyer, and the receiving lawyer in good faith reviews the materials before the lawyer knows that they were inadvertently sent, the receiving lawyer commits no ethical violation by retaining and using those materials. See D.C. Legal Ethics Committee Opinion 256.[19]

By this comment, D.C. Rule 4.4(b) codified D.C. Opinion 256 (May 16, 1995).[20] In Opinion 256, the D.C. Legal Ethics Committee determined that there was no prohibition on the review of privileged documents inadvertently sent by an opponent where the privileged status of the document is not apparent from the face of the document. The committee explained that in the District of Columbia, "the underlying law holds that inadvertently disclosed information is no longer protected." As a result, "there would appear to be no justification for requiring the receiving lawyer to accord it special treatment." The committee added that if it were in a jurisdiction where an inadvertent disclosure "does not *ipso facto* waive the attorney-client privilege," "our conclusion might be different."[21]

---

[19] Comment [3] concludes by stating that, "Whether the privileged status of a writing has been waived is a matter of law beyond the scope of these Rules. Similarly, this rule does not address the legal duties of a lawyer who receives a writing that the lawyer knows or reasonably should know may have been wrongfully obtained by the sending person. (Citation omitted.)."

[20] Http://www.dcbar.org/for_lawyers/ethics/legal_ethics/opinions/opinion256.cfm.

[21] Hopson v. Mayor and City Council of Baltimore, et al., 232 F.R.D. 228 (D. Md. 2005) discusses the case law on privilege waivers in the United States. Historically, there have been three jurisprudential approaches. Some courts have held that inadvertent production of a privileged communication is an irretrievable waiver. The First Circuit, District of Columbia Circuit, and the Federal Circuit adhere to this "strict accountability" view. *Id.* at 235. Other courts have held that unless the disclosure of the privileged information was intentional or there is gross negligence, there is no waiver. The Eighth Circuit and a number of district courts have adopted this "lenient/to err is human" approach. *Id.* at 235-36. The remaining courts that have addressed the topic have taken a middle ground. They look at the facts to determine the circumstances of the disclosure, and they evaluate the reaction of the producing party to the discovery of the production. The more careless the production and the more dilatory the response to obtain return of privileged information, the more likely a court would determine that the privilege was waived. *Id.* at 236. In May 2007, the United States Advisory Committee on the Federal Rules of Evidence proposed Fed. R. Evid. 502, which provides in part that an inadvertent disclosure does *not* operate as a waiver in a federal *or a state* proceeding if the holder of the privilege or work product protection "took reasonable steps to prevent disclosure" and "reasonable and prompt steps to rectify the

D.C. Opinion 341 extends the right to view metadata associated with an electronic document where there is no actual prior knowledge that the production was inadvertent. The committee explained:

> Given the ubiquitous exchange of electronic documents and the sending lawyers' obligation to avoid inadvertent productions of metadata,[22] we believe that mere uncertainty by the receiving lawyer as to the inadvertence of the sender does not trigger an ethical obligation by the receiving lawyer to refrain from reviewing the metadata. This standard is consistent with our conclusion in Opinion No. 256.

How cautious must receiving lawyers be? If a document is obviously privileged, can a lawyer working under the D.C. rules of professional conduct claim he or she reviewed the materials in "good faith" before learning of the inadvertence? Opinion 341 offers three guidelines to receiving lawyers:

1. If the sending lawyer tells the receiving lawyer of the inadvertent production of privileged information before the receiving lawyer reviews the information, obviously the receiving lawyer has prior actual knowledge.
2. "Such actual knowledge may also exist where a receiving lawyer immediately notices upon review of the metadata that it is clear that protected information was unintentionally included." The opinion gives the example of metadata that represents a candid exchange between an adverse party and its lawyer that is a privileged communication "on its face."

---

error" including, if applicable, following Fed. R. Civ. P. 26(b)(5)(B). This is a fact-specific inquiry to be made on a case-by-case basis. Fed. R. Evid. 502 would also protect the privilege and preclude waiver claims by third parties if production is made to an opponent in litigation under a "quick peek" or "clawback" agreement as long as there is a court order providing such protection. *See* http://www.uscourts.gov/rules/Reports/EV05-2007.pdf. Fed. R. Evid. 502 had to be approved by Congress. *Id.* On February 27, 2008, S. 2450, which adopts Rule 502, was passed in the Senate and on September 8, it was approved by the House. The president signed the legislation on September 19, 2008, making Rule 502 effective immediately in future proceedings and "where practicable" in pending proceedings. *See* http://www.govtrack.us/congress/bill.xpd?bill=s110-2450. With the adoption of Rule 502, the D.C. Legal Ethics Committee may be revisiting Opinion 341. *See also* Barkett, *The Pieces to the Privilege Protection Puzzle*, 22 N.R.E. 50 (Fall 2007) for a discussion of the relationship between Model Rule 4.4, Fed. R. Civ. P. 26(b)(5)(B), and Fed. R. Evid. 502.

[22] The D.C. committee was referring to the lawyer's obligations under Model Rule 1.6, discussed below.

3. "[A] prudent receiving lawyer who is uncertain whether the sender intended to include particular information should contact the sending lawyer to inquire."[23]

In a litigation setting, the D.C. Legal Ethics Committee reached a similar conclusion that requires explanation to understand the presumptions upon which it relied. In its analysis, the committee cited *Williams v. Sprint/United Mgmt.*, 230 F.R.D. 640 (D. Kan. 2005). Without prior court

[23] One could argue that this last suggestion controls the inquiry. Prudent lawyers will not want to risk being disqualified by learning of privileged information that they had an ethical obligation to avoid. *Cf.* Rico, et al. v. Mitsubishi Motors Corp., et al., 42 Cal. 4th 807, 171 P.3d 1092 (2007). In this case, the California Supreme Court disqualified counsel who had reviewed privileged information. The court set forth this rule: "'When a lawyer who receives materials that obviously appear to be subject to an attorney-client privilege or otherwise clearly appear to be confidential and privileged and where it is reasonably apparent that the materials were provided or made available through inadvertence, the lawyer receiving such materials should refrain from examining the materials any more than is essential to ascertain if the materials are privileged, and shall immediately notify the sender that he or she possesses material that appears to be privileged. The parties may then proceed to resolve the situation by agreement or may resort to the court for guidance with the benefit of protective orders and other judicial intervention as may be justified.'" 171 P.3d at 1099 (*quoting from* State Comp. Ins. Fund v. WPS, Inc., 70 Cal. App. 4th 644, 656-57 (1999)). In affirming the trial court's order of disqualification, it then held that the damage caused by the receiving lawyer's "dissemination and use" of the document was "unmitigable." The case had unusual facts. The document in question (defense counsel's typed copy of notes, not marked as confidential or work product, on a meeting with experts about defendant's vulnerability in this rollover products liability action) was left by defense counsel in a conference room during a deposition break. Plaintiffs' counsel remained in the room. Plaintiffs' counsel said he received the document from the court reporter. The court reporter did not recall seeing the document or giving exhibits or documents to an attorney. The trial court found that the defendant had failed to prove that plaintiff's counsel had taken the document from defense counsel's file and, therefore, concluded that the document came into plaintiff's possession inadvertently. *See also* Atlas Air, Inc. v. Traurig, 2008 WL 4224398 (Fla. 3rd DCA Sept. 17, 2008) where a third-party contractor was retained by the parties to copy and produce documents inspected by the parties lawyers' for production to the defendant. The contractor accidentally included plaintiffs' privileged documents in preparing a computer disc of what apparently were scanned documents for production. The lead lawyer at the law firm representing defendant reviewed the disc, saw the privileged documents, and reviewed several of the documents. At least one other lawyer in the firm had reviewed at least one of the privileged documents as well. Plaintiff learned what happened and moved to disqualify not only the lead lawyer but also the law firm. The lead lawyer was disqualified but the firm was not. By discretionary writ, plaintiff petitioned the appellate court which reversed. It ordered the law firm disqualified as well because of the potential that the law firm had gained a tactical advantage by viewing the privileged documents.

approval, defendant had removed formulas (i.e., metadata) in Excel spreadsheets it produced after the magistrate judge had issued a pretrial order requiring production in native format. The magistrate judge held that production in native format had to include metadata unless the party objected, the parties agreed not to produce metadata, or the party sought a protective order.[24] The committee cited the case for the proposition that metadata may be probative evidence in litigation.

The committee also identified Fed. R. Civ. P. 26(f) and other e-discovery changes to the Federal Rules of Civil Procedure to make the point that parties in federal court are required to discuss the nature of electronic documents in their possession, the manner in which they are maintained, and the form of production—including discussion of metadata and privilege issues with respect to "some or all of the metadata."

While conceding that the federal rules had no application in D.C. courts, the D.C. Legal Ethics Committee determined that because of the

[24] The committee did not cite a later *Williams* opinion, where the same magistrate judge refused to require production of metadata for certain electronically stored information because the requesting party could not justify a need for it. Williams v. Sprint/United Management Co., 2006 WL 3691604, *14 (D. Kan. Dec. 12, 2006): "Previously, this Court has ordered Defendant to produce the Excel RIF spreadsheets in native format, but in that instance Plaintiffs provided valid reasons for the spreadsheets to be produced in their native format. Namely, that the contents of the spreadsheet cells could not otherwise be viewed as the cells contained formulas. Also, in many instances, the column width of the cells prevented viewing of the entire content of the cells. Here, other than arguing that ordering Defendant to reproduce the transmittal e-mails together with their attachments in native format would be more helpful to Plaintiffs in matching up the transmittal e-mails with their respective attachments, Plaintiffs fail to provide any other reason why they need the transmittal e-mails produced in their native format. For these reasons, the Court denies Plaintiffs' request for Defendant to produce all its RIF-related transmittal e-mails in native format with all attachments in native format and attached to the transmittal e-mails." There appears to be a growing movement in federal courts to require "particularized need" before permitting production of metadata. *See, e.g.*, Wyeth v. Impax Labs, 2006 U.S. Dist. LEXIS 79761 (D. Del. Oct. 26, 2006); Kentucky Speedway, LLC v. Nat'l Assoc. of Stock Car Auto Racing, Inc., 2006 U.S. Dist. LEXIS 92028 (E.D. Ky. Dec. 18, 2006). Illustratively, the United States District Court for the District of Delaware has adopted default standards for e-discovery that are applicable where the parties cannot agree on e-discovery issues. For the format of production, the Delaware District Court default standards provide that, in the absence of agreement, metadata must be preserved but need not be produced unless a "particularized need" is shown. *See* http://www.ded.uscourts.gov/Announce/Policies/Policy01.htm (Default Standard 6 (D. Del.)). Citing *Speedway*, the D.C. Legal Ethics Committee disclaimed any endorsement of the holding in *Williams* (cited in the text) and said it was not seeking to provide guidance with respect to the rules of discovery. D.C. Ethics Op. 341, n.7.

"obligations of a sending lawyer in providing electronic documents in response to a discovery request or a subpoena," and because the scope of protection in a discovery context is limited "to material which falls within an evidentiary privilege," a receiving lawyer "is generally justified in assuming that metadata was provided intentionally."[25] In what appears to be after-the-fact logic, the committee also found support in its determination by relying on D.C. Rules 1.1 and 1.3,[26] saying that a lawyer had "an obligation competently and diligently to review, use, and preserve the evidence."[27]

However, even in a litigation context, relying on D.C. Rule 8.4,[28] the committee decided that if a receiving lawyer "has actual knowledge that metadata containing protected information was inadvertently sent by the sending lawyer," as was the case in D.C. Ethics Opinion 256, the receiving lawyer must advise the sending lawyer and "determine whether such protected information was disclosed inadvertently."

---

[25] As was the case in Maryland Ethics Docket No. 2007-09, and also citing Rules 1.2 and 1.4, the D.C. Legal Ethics Committee added that a lawyer did not have to exercise its ethical right to review privileged documents that the lawyer did not know were inadvertently produced: "By this conclusion, we do not imply that a lawyer must retain and/or use inadvertently disclosed materials that are not subject of ethical restraints. As a matter of courtesy or reciprocity, a lawyer may decline to retain or use documents that the lawyer might otherwise be entitled to use, although (depending on the significance of the documents) this might be a matter on which consultation with the client may be necessary. *See* Rules 1.2(a) and 1.4(b)."

[26] I discuss Model Rule 1.3 below.

[27] Bright lines have value in ethical analyses. The D.C. Legal Ethics Committee appears to be creating confusion by basing an ethical analysis on a discovery response under the federal rules. Those same federal rules recognize how, in an electronic world, inadvertent production is a likely event. In its Note to Fed. R. Civ. P. 26(f), the Advisory Committee explained why privilege concerns can become "more acute" when electronically stored information is sought. "The volume of such data, and the informality that attends use of e-mail and some other types of electronically stored information, may make privilege determinations more difficult, and privilege review correspondingly more expensive and time consuming. Other aspects of electronically stored information pose particular difficulties for privilege review. For example, production may be sought of information automatically included in electronic document files but not apparent to the creator of the document or to readers. Computer programs may retain draft language, editorial comments, and other deleted matter (sometimes referred to as 'embedded data' or 'embedded edits') in an electronic document file but not make them apparent to the reader. Information describing the history, tracking, or management of an electronic document (sometimes called 'metadata') is usually not apparent to the reader viewing a hard copy or screen image." 2005 Adv. Comm. Report, p. 33–34.

[28] I discuss Model Rule 8.4 below.

> If the sender advises that the protected information was unintentionally provided, then the receiving lawyer should follow the directives of the sending lawyer regarding the disposition of the electronic document. Under these circumstances, however, the receiving lawyer is permitted to take protective measures to ensure that potential evidence is not destroyed and to preserve the right to challenge the claim that the information is privileged or otherwise not subject to discovery and obtain an adjudication on that point. Of course, this is all subject to applicable rules of procedure and court orders that may otherwise govern.

D.C. Ethics Op. 341.

Arizona Bar Committee on the Rules of Professional Conduct Opinion 07-03: Mining of Metadata Impermissible

The Committee on the Rules of Professional Conduct of the Arizona Bar agreed with the Florida position in Arizona Opinion 07-03 (November 2007).[29] In that opinion on the scope of Arizona RPC 4.4(b), the committee specifically disagreed with D.C. Ethics Opinion 341[30] in reaching the conclusion that if a "recipient discovers metadata by any means, and knows or reasonably should know that the sender did not intend to transmit the information, the recipient has a duty to follow the procedures set forth in ER 4.4(b)."[31] Arizona's Rule 4.4(b) differs from Model

---

[29] Http://www.myazbar.org/Ethics/opinionview.cfm?id=695.

[30] In note 1, the Arizona committee explained: "The District of Columbia, in Op. 341 (September 2007), held that '[a] receiving lawyer is prohibited from reviewing metadata sent by an adversary *only* where he has actual knowledge that the metadata was inadvertently sent.' (Emphasis added). While Op. 341 may reflect an effort to reach a middle ground between the position of the ABA, on the one hand, and the positions of Alabama, Florida, and New York on the other hand, we respectfully disagree with the District of Columbia. Subject to the specific exceptions described elsewhere in this opinion, a lawyer who receives an electronic communication should not be engaged in the intentional examination of the document's metadata in the first place and, in our view, would bear the burden of establishing that any such intentional examination was for a proper purpose and not for the purpose of attempting to discover any confidential or privileged information that might be contained therein." The New York and Alabama opinions referred to in the quote are discussed below.

[31] The Arizona committee discussed an exception to this rule: "A lawyer who receives an electronic communication may attempt to discover the metadata that is embedded therein if he or she has the consent of the sender, or if such conduct is allowed by a rule, order, or procedure of a court or other applicable provision of law. Even so, if the lawyer comes across information that the lawyer knows or reasonably should know was not intended to be transmitted by the sender, the recipient has a duty to follow the procedures set forth in ER 4.4(b)."

Rule 4.4(b), and that difference explains—at least in part—why the Arizona committee disagreed with the ABA Standing Committee's position in ABA Ethics Opinion 06-442:

> We also note that there is a significant difference between the Model Rules of Professional Conduct as promulgated by the ABA and the Rules of Professional Conduct as adopted by the Arizona Supreme Court. Under Arizona's version of ER 4.4(b), a "lawyer who receives a document and knows or reasonably should know that the document was inadvertently sent shall promptly notify the sender and preserve the status quo for a reasonable period of time in order to permit the sender to take protective measures." While it might be argued that ER 4.4(b) is inapplicable because the document was not inadvertently sent, only the metadata embedded therein, we think that is an insubstantial distinction. If the document as sent contains metadata that reveals confidential or privileged information, it was not sent in the form in which it was intended to be sent, and the harm intended to be remedied by ER 4.4(b) is the same. Therefore, a lawyer who receives an electronic document from another party, and who discovers metadata embedded in the document that the lawyer knows or reasonably should know is revealing confidential or privileged information, has a duty to notify the sender and to preserve the status quo for a reasonable period of time in order to permit the sender to take protective measures. ER 4.4(b).[32]

Arizona Ethics Opinion 07-03 has an alternative ground in support of its result, echoing ethics opinions from New York and Alabama whose

[32] As is the case with all of the ethics opinions discussed herein that address the subject, the Arizona committee added: "We express no opinion on whether any evidentiary privilege continues to exist once an inadvertent disclosure has occurred, or whether the lawyer has incurred civil liability as the result of such disclosure. Those are questions of substantive law." F.R. Evid. 502 which went into effect on September 19, 2008, applies to state court proceedings. Specifically, F.R. Evid. 502(c) provides that a disclosure of privileged or protected information made in a state court proceeding that is not the subject of a state-court order concerning waiver does *not* operate as a waiver in a federal proceeding as long as the disclosure: (1) "would not be a waiver under this rule if it had been made in a federal proceeding; or (2) is not a waiver under the law of the state where the disclosure occurred." F.R.Evid. 502(b) provides that an inadvertent disclosure of privileged or protected information does *not* operate as a waiver in a federal or a state proceeding if the holder of the privilege or work product protection "took reasonable steps to prevent disclosure" and the holder "took reasonable and prompt steps to rectify the error" including (if applicable) following F.R.Civ.P. 26(b)(5)(B), which, as discussed earlier, deals with the steps a recipient of inadvertently-produced privileged documents must take if notified by a sender of the inadvertent production.

authors agree with the position taken by the Florida Bar that metadata mining is ethically improper but under a different rationale. But to explain why, I must first discuss Model Rule 8.4.

The Breadth of "Professional Misconduct" Under Model Rule 8.4

Model Rule 8.4 defines "professional misconduct." It provides in pertinent part:

> It is professional misconduct for a lawyer to:
>
> (a) violate or attempt to violate the Rules of Professional Conduct, knowingly assist or induce another to do so, or do so through the acts of another;
> (b) commit a criminal act that reflects adversely on the lawyer's honesty, trustworthiness or fitness as a lawyer in other respects;
> (c) engage in conduct involving dishonesty, fraud, deceit or misrepresentation;
> (d) engage in conduct that is prejudicial to the administration of justice; . . .

Model Rule 8.4(a) should not surprise anyone. If a lawyer violates the Rules of Professional Conduct, that is by definition "professional misconduct." I do not assume that a lawyer will commit a criminal act in addressing e-discovery issues. Phrased another way, if a lawyer does commit a crime in an e-discovery context, the lawyer's problems are much larger than facing a bar grievance.

Model Rule 8.4(c) should never be taken lightly. "Dishonesty, fraud, and deceit" are powerful words and I will assume that no lawyer will engage in any of these in an e-discovery context. But does a "misrepresentation" require "intent" to deceive, or can a misrepresentation be negligent?[33] Comment [2] to Rule 8.4(c) perhaps sheds a hint of light on the word by focusing on offenses that relate to characteristics "relevant to law practice":

> Although a lawyer is personally answerable to the entire criminal law, a lawyer should be professionally answerable only for offenses that indicate lack of those characteristics relevant to law practice.

[33] Model Rule 1.0(d) defines "fraud" or "fraudulent" as denoting "conduct that is fraudulent under the substantive or procedural law of the applicable jurisdiction and has a purpose to deceive." "Misrepresentation" is not defined in Rule 1.0.

> Offenses involving violence, dishonesty, breach of trust, or serious interference with the administration of justice are in that category.

Unlike an intentional misrepresentation, a negligent misrepresentation may not constitute a "breach of trust" or "dishonesty." A misstatement left uncorrected might, however, assume the characteristics of an intentional misrepresentation. Misstatements can occur in an e-discovery context because of poor communication or miscommunication between the lawyer and his or her client. They also can be due to misunderstandings regarding, among other things, the architecture of the client's electronically stored information, required forms of production, the length of time information is kept in accessible storage media before being moved to a backup tape, how long backup tapes are maintained, what protocols are followed to retain information when an employee is separated from employment, the scope of key players, and the storage habits of key players. I assume, however, that a prudent lawyer who discovers that a misstatement has been made will promptly make a correction.[34]

Comment [2] also refers to "serious interference" with "the administration of justice." Is the comment attempting to modify Model Rule 8.4(d), or does "serious interference with" mean the same as "prejudicial to" in the "administration of justice"? If there is a difference, the language of the rule should be controlling.

Let's return to whether it is ethical for a lawyer to mine metadata in documents received from an adversary. From the discussion of Model Rule 4.4, we know that the ethics opinion writers for the ABA, Maryland,

[34] That assumption may not be correct. In Qualcomm Inc. v. Broadcom Corp., 2008 WL 66932 (S.D. Calif. Jan. 7, 2008), Qualcomm's trial counsel, during trial on January 18, 2007, argued at a sidebar conference against the admission of an e-mail list. Broadcom believed that persons on the list received e-mails that would establish Broadcom's defense to Qualcomm's claim of patent infringement. Qualcomm's counsel told the trial judge, however, that "there are no emails . . . there's no evidence that any email was actually sent to this list." *Id.* However, just four days before, another of Qualcomm's trial attorneys had discovered twenty-one e-mails sent to a Qualcomm witness whose name was on the e-mail list. As the magistrate judge later observed as part of her order awarding Broadcom an $8.5 million sanction against Qualcomm, "None of the Qualcomm attorneys who were present during the sidebar mentioned" the twenty-one e-mails found just a few days earlier. *Id.* at *4. The witness later testified. During cross examination by Broadcom's counsel, she revealed the presence of the twenty-one e-mails. After initial objection, Qualcomm ultimately produced the twenty-one e-mails, which apparently were material since the jury returned a verdict in Broadcom's favor on its defense. *Id.* at *5. There is no indication in the opinion that the misstatement was corrected. As discussed below, Model Rule 3.3(a) requires the correction of misstatements made to a tribunal.

and the District of Columbia say "yes" (each for different reasons) and the Florida Bar says "no." None of these opinions mention Model Rule 8.4 or its state law equivalents.

To date, three state bars—New York, Alabama, and Arizona—and one county bar association—New York—have relied on Model Rule 8.4(d) or its equivalent Model Code provision, in concluding that this conduct is prohibited.

New York Bar Committee on Professional Ethics Opinions 749 and 782: Mining of Metadata Impermissible

In its Opinion 749 (December 14, 2001),[35] the Committee on Professional Ethics of the New York State Bar Association (NYSBA) addressed metadata before the use of the word was in vogue. The committee faced this problem:

> Modern computer technology enables sophisticated users who receive documents by electronic transmission to "get behind" what is visible on the computer screen and determine, among other things, revisions made at various stages, and sometimes even the authors of the revisions. Use of this technology would enable a lawyer who receives e-mail and electronic documents from counsel for an opposing party to obtain various kinds of information that the sender has not intentionally made available to the lawyer. For example, a lawyer who has received the final draft of a contract from counsel for a party with whom the lawyer is negotiating would be able to see prior drafts of the contract and, perhaps, learn the identity of those who made the revisions, without the knowledge or consent of the sending lawyer.

The committee determined that this conduct violated New York's Model Code:

> The Code prohibits a lawyer from engaging in conduct "involving dishonesty, fraud, deceit or misrepresentation," DR 1-102(A)(4) and "conduct that is prejudicial to the administration of justice." DR 1-102(A)(5). We believe that in light of the strong public policy in favor of preserving confidentiality as the foundation of the lawyer-client relationship, use of technology to surreptitiously obtain information that may be protected by the attorney-client privilege, the work product doctrine or that may otherwise constitute a "secret"

---

[35] Http://www.nysba.org/AM/Template.cfm?Section=Ethics_Opinions&TEMPLATE=/CM/ContentDisplay.cfm&CONTENTID=6533.

> of another lawyer's client would violate the letter and spirit of these Disciplinary Rules.

The committee's Opinion Number 782 (December 8, 2004)[36] echoed the holding in Opinion 749. In referring to the obligations of a lawyer who receives inadvertently produced privileged information, the committee this time used the word "metadata" when it discussed the holding in Opinion 749:

> Lawyer-recipients also have an obligation not to exploit an inadvertent or unauthorized transmission of client confidences or secrets. In N.Y. State 749, we concluded that the use of computer technology to access client confidences and secrets revealed in metadata constitutes an "impermissible intrusion on the attorney-client relationship in violation of the Code."[37]

New York County Lawyers' Association Opinion 738: Mining of Metadata Impermissible

The New York County Lawyers' Association (NYCLA) reached the same result in its Ethics Opinion 738 (March 24, 2008).[38] The NYCLA's Committee on Professional Ethics specifically disagreed with the ABA's position.[39] Relying in part on NYSBA Ethics Opinion 749, and addressing only a nonlitigation setting, the committee concluded:

---

[36] Http://www.nysba.org/AM/Template.cfm?Section=Ethics_Opinions&TEMPLATE=/CM/ContentDisplay.cfm&CONTENTID=13630.

[37] On November 3, 2007, the New York State Bar Association's House of Delegates approved a report containing New York's proposed Rules of Professional Conduct. The proposed rules, dated February 1, 2008, were referred to the Presiding Justices of the Appellate Division of the Supreme Court of New York for approval. *See* http://www.nysba.org/AM/Template.cfm?Section=Professional_Standards_for_Attorneys&Template=/CM/ContentDisplay.cfm&ContentID=15179. If adopted, New York would join the forty-seven other states, which together with the District of Columbia have adopted the Model Rules in whole or in substantial part. New York's proposed Rule 8.4(c) and (d) are identical to Model Rule 8.4(c) and (d).

[38] Http://www.nycla.org/siteFiles/Publications/Publications1154_0.pdf.

[39] The committee explained that mistakes can occur and an attorney "may neglect on occasion to scrub or properly send an electronic document. The question here is whether opposing counsel is permitted to take advantage of the sending attorney's mistake and hunt for the metadata that was improperly left in the document." Its answer was "no." "This Committee finds that the NYSBA rule is a better interpretation of the Code's disciplinary rules and ethical considerations and New York precedents than the ABA's opinion on this issue. Thus, this Committee concludes that when a lawyer sends opposing counsel correspondence or other material with metadata, the receiving attorney may not ethically

> A lawyer who receives from an adversary electronic documents that appear to contain inadvertently produced metadata is ethically obligated to avoid searching the metadata in those documents. While attorneys are advised to take due care in sending correspondence, contracts, or other documents to opposing counsel by scrubbing the documents to ensure that they are free of metadata, an adversary may not ethically take advantage of a breach in the attorney's care by intentionally searching for metadata. Using the metadata is unethical if the recipient's intent is to investigate opposing counsel's work product or client confidences or secrets or if the recipient is likely to find opposing counsel's work product or client confidences or secrets by searching the metadata. Without a prior understanding to the contrary, there is a presumption that disclosure of metadata is inadvertent and would be unethical to view.

Alabama Bar Office of General Counsel Ethics Opinion 2007-02: Mining of Metadata Impermissible

In its Ethics Opinion 2007-02 (March 14, 2007),[40] the Alabama Bar Office of General Counsel (OGC) adopted the position of the NYSBA's Opinion 749 and, relying on Alabama RPC 8.4,[41] held:

> The mining of metadata constitutes a knowing and deliberate attempt by the recipient attorney to acquire confidential and privileged information in order to obtain an unfair advantage against an opposing party.

Perhaps taking a cue from D.C. Ethics Opinion 341,[42] the Alabama Bar OGC, however, suggested that one "possible" exception to this prohibition on metadata mining "involves electronic discovery." Mindful of the promulgation of rules of civil procedure governing the rights and obligations of litigants, the Alabama Bar OGC demurred to those court rules:

---

search the metadata in those electronic documents with the intent to find privileged material or if finding privileged material is likely to occur from the search."

[40] *See* http://www.lexisnexis.com/applieddiscovery/lawLibrary/courtRules.asp#Bar.

[41] Alabama Rules of Prof'l Conduct R. 8.4 is identical to Model Rule 8.4.

[42] As discussed above, the D.C. Legal Ethics Committee in Opinion 341 distinguished between mining metadata in litigation and nonlitigation contexts, suggesting that there was a presumption "generally" in the former case that production of privileged metadata was intentional. Alabama Ethics Op. 2007-02 does not, however, cite the D.C Ethics Op. 341.

> The production of metadata during discovery will ordinarily be a legal matter within the sole discretion of the courts. The Commission advises attorneys, however, to be cognizant of the issue of disclosing metadata during discovery. Both parties should seek direction from the court in determining whether a document's metadata is to be produced during discovery.

Rule 8.4 Under D.C. (341), Arizona (07-03), and Maryland (2007-09) Ethics Opinions

The D.C. Bar Legal Ethics Committee does agree with New York and Alabama on the application of Rule 8.4 when a lawyer "wrongfully" mines metadata. D.C. Ethics Opinion 341. But "wrongful mining" occurs under the D.C. RPC only when the lawyer knows that the metadata were inadvertently provided:

> In our view, however, Rule 8.4 is implicated only when the receiving lawyer has actual prior knowledge that the metadata was inadvertently provided. Given the ubiquitous exchange of electronic documents and the sending lawyers' obligation to avoid inadvertent productions of metadata, we believe that mere uncertainty by the receiving lawyer as to the inadvertence of the sender does not trigger an ethical obligation by the receiving lawyer to refrain from reviewing the metadata.

Id.

The Arizona Committee on the Rules of Professional Conduct, in its Opinion 07-03,[43] relied on Arizona RPC 8.4, Alabama Ethics Opinion 2007-02, and the fundamental principle of confidentiality in the lawyer-client relationship, in concluding that:

> Lawyers, in light of this fundamental principle, and in keeping with their status as members of a learned profession, should refrain from conduct that amounts to an unjustified intrusion into the client-lawyer relationship that exists between the opposing party and his or her counsel. ER 8.4(a)-(d). See also Ala. Op. RO-2007-02.

The Arizona committee also directly attacked the logic of the ABA Standing Committee's decision in ABA Ethics Opinion 06-442. The ABA Standing Committee had rejected the reasoning of NYSBA Ethics

[43] As a reminder, the opinion can be found at http://www.myazbar.org/Ethics/opinionview.cfm?id=695.

Opinions 749 and 782. It had determined that a receiving lawyer who mines metadata does not violate Model Rule 8.4 and that Model Rule 4.4 was the sole Model Rule that addressed the subject of the conduct of the receiving lawyer. The ABA Standing Committee added that sending lawyers could figure out a way to "scrub" metadata before production or might only send hard copy or an image of a document, or should negotiate a confidentiality agreement or, if in litigation, a protective order to permit the sending lawyer to "pull back"[44] privileged information. The Arizona committee rejected this rationale:

> The American Bar Association (ABA), in Formal Op. 06-442 (August 5, 2006), concluded that the Model Rules of Professional Conduct do not prohibit such conduct. We respectfully decline to follow the

---

[44] In the Note to Fed. R. Civ. P. 26(f), the Advisory Committee suggested protocols that parties may employ to minimize the risk of waiver of any privilege or protection. "They may agree that the responding party will provide the requested materials for initial examination without waiving any privilege—sometimes known as a 'quick peek.'" After reviewing what the requesting party designates for production, the producing party then asserts a privilege under Fed. R. Civ. P. 26(b)(5)(a) describing the nature of documents or information not produced in a manner that allows other parties to assess the applicability of privilege or protection (even though the requesting party's counsel will have already seen the document or information). "On other occasions, parties enter agreements—sometimes called 'clawback agreements'—providing that production without intent to waive privilege should not be a waiver so long as the producing party identifies the documents mistakenly produced, and that the documents should be returned under those circumstances." 2005 Adv. Comm. Report, p. 34. *See* Rowe Entertainment, Inc. v. The William Morris Agency, Inc., et al., 205 F.R.D. 421, 432-33 (S.D.N.Y. 2002), where the magistrate judge proposed a "clawback" procedure so that the privilege could be asserted by the responding party after production and review of electronic documents by the requesting party. A motion to reverse the magistrate judge's order on cost-shifting was denied by the district court. 2002 U.S. Dist. LEXIS 8308 (S.D. N.Y. May 8, 2002). *Cf.* Zenith Electronics Corp. v. WH-TV Broadcasting Corp., 2004 U.S. Dist. LEXIS (N.D. Ill. 2004) (where the district court apparently ordered a clawback procedure in response to a requesting party's motion to compel where the requesting party's proposed protocol called for a consultant to review the electronic files, identify what was to be produced, and then responding parties could review those files for privilege and identify the files to be redacted on privilege grounds. The district court's order invited counsel to file an emergency motion if problems arose under the protocol). *See also* J.C. Assocs. v. Fidelity & Guaranty Ins. Co., 2005 WL 1570140 (D.D.C. July 2005) (where plaintiff sought claims files that defendant estimated might total 1.3 million files, and plaintiff then focused on a geographic subset of 448 files, the magistrate judge proposed a quick-peek and clawback protective order and gave defendant ten days to determine whether it would surrender the 428 files on this basis). Fed. R. Evid. 502 now protects parties who enter into clawback agreements from waiver claims by third parties if the agreement is embodied in a court order.

> ABA position. Despite the most reasonable and thorough precautions, and even with the best of intentions, it may not be possible for the sending lawyer to be absolutely certain that all of the potentially harmful metadata has been "scrubbed" from the document before it is transmitted electronically. Under the ABA position, the sending lawyer would be at the mercy of the recipient lawyer. Under such circumstances, the sending lawyer might conclude that the only ethically safe course of action is to forego the use of electronic document transmission entirely. We do not think that is realistic or necessary. Under the position adopted by Florida, New York, Alabama, and now Arizona, the sending lawyer is alerted to the potential problem and is reminded of the duty to take reasonable steps to prevent the inadvertent disclosure of confidential or privileged information. At the same time, except in the specific circumstances described below, the recipient lawyer has a corresponding duty not to "mine" the document for metadata that may be embedded therein or otherwise engage in conduct which amounts to an unjustified intrusion into the client-lawyer relationship that exists between the opposing party and his or her counsel.

There is one other twist to this metadata-mining conundrum, involving the question of whether a violation of rules of civil procedure also is a violation of Rule 8.4(d). If a lawyer fails to advise a client of a duty to preserve electronically stored information, and material information prejudicial to the opposing party is lost as a result, does this conduct represent a Rule 8.4(d) violation because the administration of justice has been prejudiced? Probably not. The Federal Rules of Civil Procedure do not explicitly impose an obligation on a lawyer to advise a client of the client's duty to preserve.[45]

---

[45] However, lawyers engaged to represent clients in litigation know that a duty to preserve exists and must be in a position to offer appropriate counsel on the trigger date of the duty to preserve because of the potential for sanctions under the federal rules should the client fail to honor preservation obligations. Depending on the scope of the engagement or on the circumstances, the failure to give advice that a duty to preserve exists could have legal consequences. Comment [20] to the "Scope" of the Model Rules provides that violation of a Model Rule should not itself give rise to a cause of action against a lawyer or create any presumption in such a case that a legal duty has been breached. It adds that the Rules of Professional Conduct are not designed to be a basis for civil liability. The end of this comment, however, adds: "Nevertheless, since the Rules do establish standards of conduct by lawyers, a lawyer's violation of a Rule may be evidence of breach of the applicable standard of conduct." Lawyers should be mindful of this admonition in evaluating risks associated with their interpretation of, and conduct under, the Model Rules.

But the federal rules do require a lawyer to return, sequester, or destroy documents if notified by the sender that privileged documents were sent inadvertently. Fed. R. Civ. P. 26(b)(5)(B). If a lawyer fails in this obligation, does the lawyer violate Model Rule 8.4(d)?

As discussed above in connection with Model Rule 4.4(b), in Ethics Docket 2007-09, the Maryland State Bar Association Committee on Ethics determined that a lawyer could review and use metadata without first ascertaining whether it was inadvertently transmitted. The committee based its conclusion in large measure on Maryland's failure to adopt Model Rule 4.4(b). The Maryland committee, however, also explained that the e-discovery amendments to the federal rules were designed to foster agreements on production and privilege issues associated with electronic documents. The committee acknowledged that "any such agreements would supersede" Maryland's ethical standards, except that if a lawyer failed to honor the agreement, "the attorney could well be in violation of Rule 8.4(d)[46] by engaging in conduct that is prejudicial to the administration of justice."

The Maryland Ethics Committee then quoted Fed. R. Civ. P. 26(b)(5)(B), which, as discussed above, identifies the obligations imposed on a recipient of privileged information after notice is given by the sender that such information is privileged. The committee added this exception to its conclusion that metadata mining is permissible, relying also on Maryland RPC 8.4(d):

> Accordingly, the lack of any ethical prohibition concerning the review and/or use of metadata discussed earlier in this Opinion would, at least in the arena of federal litigation, be superseded by the legal requirements set forth in the Federal Rules which go into effect on December 1, 2006, and any violation of those Federal Rules would in all likelihood[47] constitute a violation of Rule 8.4(d) as being prejudicial to the administration of justice.

At least to a certain degree, e-discovery ethics may, indeed, be superseded by rules of civil procedure as states complete the process of adopting

---

[46] The opinion reads "8.4(b)" but that is a typographical error, since Maryland Rule of Professional Conduct 8.4(d) references conduct that is prejudicial to the administration of justice.

[47] The phrase "in all likelihood" should not give lawyers comfort. Even if a failure by a lawyer to destroy, return, or sequester documents after receipt of notice under Fed. R. Civ. P. 26(b)(5)(B) is not a violation of Rule 8.4(d), it still may be sanctionable conduct under the Federal Rules of Civil Procedure.

e-discovery amendments on the heels of the federal e-discovery rules amendments. But where compliance with rules of procedure and ethics rules overlap, no lawyer should ever want to take the risk that a judge will impose the sanction of referring the lawyer to the state bar for disciplinary proceedings.

Model Rule 1.3 and Diligent Representation

Model Rule 1.3 provides:

> A lawyer shall act with reasonable diligence and promptness in representing a client.

Comment [1] to Model Rule 1.3 adds:

> A lawyer should . . . take whatever lawful and ethical measures are required to vindicate a client's cause or endeavor. A lawyer must also act with commitment and dedication to the interests of the client and with zeal in advocacy upon the client's behalf.

Suppose that a claimant in an arbitration argues that the respondent had misrepresented a material fact causing damage to the claimant. Suppose further that the claimant inadvertently produced a privileged document that contained a comment in metadata that demonstrated that the claimant had actual knowledge of the truth of the matters alleged to have been misrepresented, supporting a defense to the claim. Does Model Rule 1.3 trump Model Rules 1.6, 4.4, and 8.4, thereby permitting the lawyer to use the privileged information to serve the interests of the lawyer's client?

The D.C. Legal Ethics Committee's answer to this question is "yes" as long as the lawyer did not know of the inadvertent production. In its Opinion 341, the committee explained: "where the privileged nature of the document is not apparent on its face, there is no obligation to refrain from reviewing it, and the duty of diligent representation under D.C. Rule 1.3 may trump confidentiality concerns." Opinion 341 drew upon Opinion 256, in which the committee explained that requiring the receiving lawyer to protect the confidentiality of inadvertently produced privileged documents would "place too much of a burden on the exercise of a lawyer's obligation to represent his client zealously and diligently" under Rule 1.3.[48]

---

[48] The D.C. Legal Ethics Committee also invoked D.C. Rule 1.7(b)(4). D.C. Rule 1.7(b)(4) prohibits a lawyer from representing a client in a matter if "the lawyer's professional judgment on behalf of the client will be or reasonably may be adversely affected by . . . the lawyer's own financial, business, property or personal interests." If the receiving lawyer

In a litigation context, the D.C. Legal Ethics Committee in Opinion 341 was even more solicitous of Rule 1.3:

> In addition, when an electronic document constitutes tangible evidence, or potential tangible evidence, the receiving lawyer has an obligation competently and diligently to review, use, and preserve the evidence. *See* D.C. Rules 1.1, 1.3. The electronic document is similar to any other tangible evidence that the lawyer is expected to review in order to advance her client's interests. Where useful, for example, the lawyer in such instances may consult with a computer expert to determine the means by which the metadata can be most fully revealed and reviewed, much as a lawyer does with a fingerprint expert.

The tension in the rules between appropriate zeal in advocacy on the one hand and, on the other, protecting client confidences inadvertently produced and avoiding the label of "dishonesty, fraud, deceit, or misrepresentation," is not likely to end anytime soon, and will vary from jurisdiction to jurisdiction as ethics committees choose which line of authority to follow.

Model Rule 1.6 and the Duty of Confidentiality

Lawyers have a duty to protect the confidences of their clients. Model Rule 1.6 contains the basic "confidentiality" obligations of lawyers. Rule 1.6(a) provides that a lawyer "shall not" reveal information "relating to the representation of a client unless the client gives informed consent,"[49]

---

were ethically prohibited from using the inadvertently produced privileged information, the committee continued, his or her professional judgment "reasonably may be adversely affected" in the matter, creating a Rule 1.7(b)(4) conflict that could require withdrawal under D.C. Rule 1.16(a). Model Rule 1.7 does not contain language comparable to that found in D.C. Rule 1.7(b)(4). The closest language in the Model Rules to D.C. Rule 1.7(b)(4) appears in Comment [8] to Model Rule 1.7, which provides: "Even where there is no direct adverseness, a conflict of interest exists if there is a significant risk that a lawyer's ability to consider, recommend or carry out an appropriate course of action for the client will be materially limited as a result of the lawyer's other responsibilities or interests." Both D.C. Rule 1.16(a) and Model Rule 1.16(a) provide that a lawyer must withdraw from representation if the representation will result in violation of the Rules of Professional Conduct.

[49] Informed consent "denotes the agreement by a person to a proposed course of conduct after the lawyer has communicated adequate information and explanation about the material risks of and reasonably available alternatives to the proposed course of conduct." Model Rule 1.0(e).

the disclosure is "impliedly authorized in order to carry out the representation,"[50] or the disclosure is permitted by Rule 1.6(b).[51]

A lawyer entrusted with a client's electronically stored information must take steps to protect it. I do not know of a lawyer who has not suffered from Microsoft Outlook's propensity automatically to fill in the e-mail address of a recipient for a sender in a hurry who types a couple of letters of a name and then does not scroll down for the list of potential recipients to identify the intended addressee. This failure to protect a client confidence is usually immediately remedied by the recipient who responds: "I don't think you intended this e-mail for me. I am immediately destroying it." After sending a "thank you" e-mail, the sender will resolve to be more careful: After all, Rule 1.6 is prescriptive unless the lawyer has received the client's informed consent to make the disclosure.

What if you are sending a third party a document that you and your client have edited? Is there a risk that metadata might reveal a client confidence? In our earlier discussions, we have studied at considerable length the inconsistent ethics opinions regarding the obligations imposed on the recipient of privileged information. What are the sender's obligations? In our earlier discussions, we have studied at considerable length the inconsistent ethics opinions regarding the obligations imposed on the recipient of privileged information. What are the sender's obligations?

It should come as no surprise that the ethics opinions published to date require lawyers sending information to take reasonable steps to maintain the confidentiality of documents in their possession.

In Formal Opinion 06-442, discussed earlier, the ABA Standing Committee cited to Comment [16] of Model Rule 1.6, which succinctly provides:

> A lawyer must act competently to safeguard information relating to the representation of a client against inadvertent or unauthorized disclosure by the lawyer or other persons who are participating in

[50] To illustrate this second exception, Comment [5] to Rule 1.6 explains that a lawyer is impliedly authorized to admit a fact that cannot be disputed or to make a disclosure that facilitates a satisfactory conclusion to a matter. Lawyers in a firm may also disclose information to each other relating to a client in the firm "unless the client has instructed that particular information be confined to specified lawyers."

[51] Rule 1.6(b) is not applicable in this context.

> the representation of the client or who are subject to the lawyer's supervision. See Rules 1.1, 5.1 and 5.3.[52]

The ethics opinions of Alabama, Arizona, the District of Columbia, Florida, Maryland, New York, and New York County, cited earlier, follow this principle as more fully described in Appendix II.

Model Rule 3.4 and Access to Evidence

Model Rule 3.4(a) provides:

> A lawyer shall not:
>
> (a) unlawfully obstruct another party's access to evidence or unlawfully alter, destroy or conceal a document or other material having potential evidentiary value. A lawyer shall not counsel or assist another person to do any such act; . . .

In its Opinion 341, the D.C. Legal Ethics Committee added a bit of a gloss to the duties of lawyers producing documents in litigation. Rather than relying on the D.C. RPC equivalent to Model Rule 1.6, the committee determined that senders of documents should be governed by D.C. RPC 3.4(a), which is worded somewhat differently from Model Rule 3.4(a). D.C. RPC 3.4(a) provides in part:

> A lawyer shall not:
>
> (a) Obstruct another party's access to evidence or alter, destroy, or conceal evidence, or counsel or assist another person to do so, if the lawyer reasonably should know that the evidence is or may be the subject of discovery or subpoena in any pending or imminent proceeding. Unless prohibited by law, a lawyer may receive physical evidence of any kind from the client or from another person.

The committee added that because "it is impermissible to alter electronic documents that constitute tangible evidence,"

> the removal of metadata may, at least in some instances, be prohibited as well. In addition to issues regarding discovery sanctions, the alteration or destruction of evidence can, under some circumstances, also constitute a crime. See D.C. Rule 3.4, Comment [4].

[52] Model Rules 5.1 and 5.3 are discussed below.

The committee recognized that there are different forms of metadata and that not all metadata should be treated alike.[53] Nonetheless, is the committee saying that metadata is "evidence"? Should the committee have left production of documents with or without metadata to the lawyers and the courts before whom they appear rather than entering an arena ill-suited for a general pronouncement in the absence of a concrete example? Lawyers governed by the D.C. RPC should be aware of this language even though the risk of sanctions would appear to be a greater worry for anyone who violates a court order or alters, destroys, or conceals evidence that is the subject of discovery, as I discuss in more detail below.

Model Rules 1.4(a)(4), 1.15(a), and 1.16(d) and the Safekeeping and Return of Client Property

Model Rule 1.4(a)(4) provides that a lawyer "shall" "promptly comply with reasonable requests for information" from a client.

Model Rule 1.15(a) provides:

> A lawyer shall hold property of clients or third persons that is in a lawyer's possession in connection with a representation separate from the lawyer's own property. Funds shall be kept in a separate account maintained in the state where the lawyer's office is situated, or elsewhere with the consent of the client or third person. Other property shall be identified as such and appropriately safeguarded. Complete records of such account funds and other property shall be kept by the lawyer and shall be preserved for a period of [five years] after termination of the representation.

Model Rule 1.16(d) provides:

> Upon termination of representation, a lawyer shall take steps to the extent reasonably practicable to protect a client's interests, such as giving reasonable notice to the client, allowing time for employment of other counsel, surrendering papers and property to which the client is entitled and refunding any advance payment of fee or expense that has not been earned or incurred. The lawyer may

[53] D.C. Ethics Op. 341, n.8. There are different forms of metadata. The *Sedona Glossary* contains definitions for Application Metadata, Document Metadata, E-mail Metadata, Embedded Metadata, File System Metadata, User-Added Metadata, and Vendor-Added Metadata. Http://www.sedonaconference.org/dltForm?did=TSCGlossary_12_07.pdf (December 2007). A request in discovery for "all metadata" would be *ipso facto* overbroad.

> retain papers relating to the client to the extent permitted by other law.

If a lawyer is managing litigation support for a client that includes the management of electronically stored information, the lawyer and the client should have a suitable arrangement for the storage, protection, and return of the electronically stored information.

File Storage in Electronic Format

As for client files, the Arizona Committee on the Rules of Professional Conduct's Opinion 07-02 (June 2007)[54] provides guidance to lawyers. It was written to address the question of file storage in electronic format and the subsequent destruction of the associated paper documents. These were the facts presented:

> Many lawyers have requested informal ethics advice about whether they may maintain current and certain closed client files as electronic images instead of as paper documents. Some have indicated they want to digitize closed client files (and then destroy the paper file) because of the increasing cost of storing files. Others have indicated that they wish to maintain only electronic images of current client files, both to save storage space and because they believe electronic images are easier to manage and organize. In both circumstances, these lawyers have inquired about their ability to maintain only digitized files and destroy the paper copies, and their associated obligations to their clients. In light of these frequent requests for informal ethics advice, the Committee on the Rules of Professional Conduct has chosen to issue this formal opinion sua sponte.

The committee determined that in "appropriate cases," a lawyer "may keep current and closed client files as electronic images in an attempt to maintain a paperless law practice or to more economically store files." However, after digitizing paper documents, a lawyer may not destroy *original* paper documents belonging to, or that were obtained from, the client, without client consent. The committee continued:

> After digitizing paper documents, a lawyer may destroy copies of paper documents that were obtained from the client unless the lawyer has reason to know that the client wants the lawyer to retain them. A lawyer has the discretion to decide whether to maintain

[54] Http://www.myazbar.org/Ethics/opinionview.cfm?id=694.

the balance of the file solely as electronic images and destroy the paper documents.

The committee made several points worth noting:

- A lawyer should determine if it is in the client's best interest to maintain a file in electronic form.
- Many cases may involve legally operative documents that should be maintained in their original form.
- A photocopy of a document may be as valuable for evidentiary purposes as the original, and a digital image of the photocopy may degrade that value.
- Lawyers have an obligation to provide clients with access to files.
- At the termination of representation, the lawyer is obligated to "take steps to the extent reasonably practicable to protect a client's interests, such as . . . surrendering documents and property to which the client is entitled . . . ."
- In addition, "[u]pon the client's request, the lawyer shall provide the client with all of the client's documents, and all documents reflecting work performed for the client."
- Lawyers must provide meaningful access. A lawyer who has chosen to store his or her client files digitally "cannot hand a disk or other storage medium to a client without confirming that the client is able to read the digitized images. If the client does not have the technological knowledge or access to a computer on which to display the electronic images, or if the client has hired substitute counsel who is in the same position as the client, the original lawyer may need to provide paper copies of the documents."
- If the lawyer has opted to store files solely as digital images for his or her own convenience, the lawyer will need to bear the cost of providing those paper copies, absent other agreed-upon arrangements.
- Although the lawyer must provide the client with meaningful access to the file, the lawyer need not obtain the client's consent to maintain solely as electronic images documents other than those provided by the client and with the considerations described above.
- The lawyer must maintain electronic images "in such a manner as will permit them to be readily and accurately convertible into paper format within a reasonable period of time."
- If a lawyer wishes to store client files solely as electronic images and not keep paper copies, "the lawyer must take reasonable steps to ensure that the digitized file is complete."

- When converting a document to a digital image, "the lawyer also must take reasonable precautions to avoid damaging the documents. With rare or difficult-to-replace documents, it should not be attempted."
- A lawyer who wishes to maintain the allowable portions of a client file solely as electronic images "must consider whether the format lends itself to long-term storage. Until the time a file may legitimately be destroyed, a lawyer who maintains that file solely as digitized images will need to use technology that permits the file to be readily and accurately retrievable. In addition, the lawyer should be familiar with or take steps to insure that the digital-storage medium is properly stored to maintain its shelf life."

See also Virginia Ethics Opinion 1818 (2005) (A client's file need not be maintained in paper form: "The Rules of Professional Conduct do not contain a provision specifically directing what items a lawyer must keep in the client's file or in what form.");[55] New Jersey Ethics Opinion 701 (2006) ("With the exception of 'property of the client' within the meaning of RPC 1.15, therefore, and with the important caveat we express below regarding confidentiality, we believe that nothing in the RPCs prevents a lawyer from archiving a client's file through use of an electronic medium such as PDF files or similar formats. The polestar is the obligation of the lawyer to engage in the representation competently, and to communicate adequately with the client and others. To the extent that new technology now enhances the ability to fulfill those obligations, it is

[55] Http://www.vacle.org/opinions/1818.htm. The Virginia Ethics Committee also added, however, that there may be reasons to maintain some paper documents: "This is not to say that there are not instances where a paper document might be required. There may be any number of circumstances where keeping an original paper document in the file is critical, for example, testamentary documents, marriage certificates, or handwriting exemplars, to name a few. Clients without access to computers would require the attorney to keep a paper file. As to file materials other than documents, such (as) physical evidence, an attorney must always safeguard, maintain and account for such items. Any other instances where lack of a physical item may prejudice the interests of the client would also mean that an exclusively electronic file would not be permissible. The committee opines that there is not a per se prohibition against electronic files in all instances. However, when making decisions as to what to keep in the file and in what form, while an attorney may consider storage expediency, those decisions must be made such that the attorney's duties of competence, diligence, and communication are not compromised. *See* Rules 1.1, 1.3, and 1.4. The preference for electronic storage cannot reduce a lawyer's obligation to fulfill these ethical duties for each client." (Parenthetical added.)

a welcome development.")[56] New York Ethics Opinion 680 (1996) (New York's Model Code permits "some records to be maintained in the form of computer images, while other records must, as the Code is now written, be retained in their original, hard-copy form").[57] *See, generally,* Geraghty, *From Paper to Kilobytes* (ABA February 2008).[58]

---

[56] Http://www.judiciary.state.nj.us/notices/ethics/ACPE_Opinion701_ElectronicStorage_12022005.pdf. The New Jersey Ethics Committee explained that documents like original wills, trusts, deeds, executed contracts, corporate bylaws, and minutes were "client property" that cannot be preserved "merely by digitizing them in electronic form." The caveat regarding confidentiality was that the lawyer had to exercise reasonable care to ensure the confidentiality of the electronic files. If entrusted to third parties, the committee had this to say about confidentiality: "We do think, however, that when client confidential information is entrusted in unprotected form, even temporarily, to someone outside the firm, it must be under a circumstance in which the outside party is aware of the lawyer's obligation of confidentiality, and is itself obligated, whether by contract, professional standards, or otherwise, to assist in preserving it. Lawyers typically use messengers, delivery services, document warehouses, or other outside vendors, in which physical custody of client sensitive documents is entrusted to them even though they are not employed by the firm. The touchstone in using 'reasonable care' against unauthorized disclosure is that: (1) the lawyer has entrusted such documents to an outside provider under circumstances in which there is an enforceable obligation to preserve confidentiality and security, and (2) use is made of available technology to guard against reasonably foreseeable attempts to infiltrate the data. If the lawyer has come to the prudent professional judgment he has satisfied both these criteria, then 'reasonable care' will have been exercised."

[57] Http://www.nysba.org/AM/Template.cfm?Section=Ethics_Opinions&CONTENTID=5689&TEMPLATE=/CM/ContentDisplay.cfm.

[58] Http://www.abanet.org/media/youraba/200802/article11.html. This article contains a good discussion of both RPC and ethics opinions on the topic of electronic storage of client information. Cf. Formal Opinion 2008-1 of the Association of the Bar of the City of New York Committee on Professional and Judicial Ethics (July 2008) (http://www.abcny.org/Publications/reports/show_html.php?rid=794) in which the committee addressed electronic document retention and storage generally, and e-mail retention and storage specifically, along with retrieval of electronic information if requested by a client and charging a client for such retrieval. The committee's concluded: "With respect to the electronic documents that the lawyer retains, the lawyer is not under an ethical obligation to organize those documents in any particular manner, or to store those documents in any particular storage medium, so long as the lawyer ensures that the manner of organization and storage does not (a) detract from the competence of the representation or (b) result in the loss of documents that the client may later need and may reasonably expect the lawyer to preserve. To those ends, electronic documents other than e-mails present less difficulty because they are frequently stored in document management systems in which they are typically coded with several identifying characteristics, making it easier to locate and assemble them later. E-mails raise more difficult organizational and storage issues. Some e-mail systems automatically delete e-mails after a period of time, so the lawyer must take affirmative steps to preserve those e-mails that the lawyer decides to save. In addition,

Length of Time to Maintain Client Files

There is not a specific amount of time that lawyers must maintain closed client files. ABA Informal Opinion 1384 (1977).[59] ("We cannot say that there is a specific time during which a lawyer must preserve all files and beyond which he is free to destroy all files. Good common sense should provide answers to most questions that arise.") Informal Opinion 1384 contains eight considerations for a lawyer trying to decide how long to maintain client files:

1. Unless the client consents, a lawyer should not destroy or discard items that clearly or probably belong to the client. Such items include those furnished to the lawyer by or in behalf of the client, the return of which could reasonably be expected by the client, and original documents (especially when not filed or recorded in the public records).
2. A lawyer should use care not to destroy or discard information that the lawyer knows or should know may still be necessary or useful in the assertion or defense of the client's position in a matter for which the applicable statutory limitations period has not expired.
3. A lawyer should use care not to destroy or discard information that the client may need, has not previously been given to the client, and is not otherwise readily available to the client, and which the client may reasonably expect will be preserved by the lawyer.
4. In determining the length of time for retention or disposition of a file, a lawyer should exercise discretion. The nature and contents of some files may indicate a need for longer retention than

e-mails generally are not coded, or otherwise organized, to facilitate their later retrieval. Thus, a practice with much to commend it is to organize saved e-mails to facilitate their later retrieval, for example, by coding them or saving them to dedicated electronic files. Otherwise, it may be exceedingly difficult and expensive for the lawyer to retrieve those e-mails, and, as discussed in this Opinion, the lawyer must not charge the client for retrieval costs that could reasonably have been avoided . . . . In New York, a client has a presumptive right to the lawyer's entire file in connection with a representation, subject to narrow exceptions. The lawyer may charge the client a reasonable fee, based on the lawyer's customary schedule, for gathering and producing electronic documents. That fee may reflect the reasonable costs of retrieving electronic documents from their storage media and reviewing those documents to determine the client's right of access. It is prudent for lawyer and client to discuss the retention, storage, and retrieval of electronic documents at the outset of the engagement and to consider memorializing their agreement in a retention letter."

[59] Http://www.abanet.org/cpr/ethicsearch/lawyer.html.

do the nature and contents of other files, based upon their obvious relevance and materiality to matters that can be expected to arise.

5. A lawyer should take special care to preserve, indefinitely, accurate and complete records of the lawyer's receipt and disbursement of trust funds.
6. In disposing of a file, a lawyer should protect the confidentiality of the contents.
7. A lawyer should not destroy or dispose of a file without screening it in order to determine that consideration has been given to the matters discussed above.
8. A lawyer should preserved, perhaps for an extended time, an index or identification of the files that the lawyer has destroyed or disposed of.

Id. See also New Jersey Ethics Opinion 692 (2001) ("We hold that such portions of the file which constitute 'property of the client' must be either returned to the client, disposed of pursuant to court order or agreement with the client, or preserved and maintained for a reasonable period of time following the conclusion of the matter. Absent an express agreement that the file be subject to destruction at an earlier point in time, the client may assume availability of the file up to a date seven years after it has been closed, at which time it may be destroyed.");[60] and Alabama Ethics Opinion 93-10 (1993) ("With regard to time, there is no specific period that constitutes 'reasonable' time. It depends on the nature of the documents in the file and the attendant circumstances.").[61]

[60] Http://lawlibrary.rutgers.edu/ethics/acpe/acp692_1.html. The New Jersey Ethics Committee added that provisions for confidentiality must be made by the lawyer: "Appropriate steps must be taken to ensure that confidential and privileged information remains protected and not available to third parties."

[61] Http://www.alabar.org/ogc/fopDisplay.cfm?oneId=76. The Alabama Ethics Committee did suggest that a lawyer should examine the file and segregate the contents into four categories: "(1) Documents that are clearly the property of the client and may be of some intrinsic value, whether delivered to the lawyer by the client or prepared by the lawyer for the client, such as wills, deeds, etc.; (2) documents which have been delivered to the lawyer by the client and which the client would normally expect to be returned to him; (3) documents from any source which may be of some future value to the client because of some future development that may or may not materialize; and, (4) documents which fall in neither of the above categories." The committee then explained that documents "which fall into category 1 should be retained for an indefinite period of time or preferably should be recorded or deposited with a court. Documents falling into categories 2 and 3 should be retained for a reasonable period of time at the end of which reasonable attempts should be

Return of Electronic Files in the Event of Substitution of Counsel

In the era of electronically stored information, what are a lawyer's obligations to provide electronic files to a departing member of the firm who will keep the client's work, or to return electronic files when a client decides to replace counsel?

In Opinion 2005-06/3 (January 2006), the New Hampshire Bar Association Ethics Committee tackled the first question.[62] A lawyer who left a law firm was going to continue to represent certain clients. The departing lawyer's former law firm held client files in both paper and electronic format. The law firm agreed to turn over paper files, including paper copies of e-mails that had been placed in files. The departing lawyer also wanted copies of all e-mail communications and electronic documents on the firm network. That request prompted the law firm to ask the New Hampshire Ethics Committee whether it could "avoid organizing thousands of electronic items in the lawyer's 'inbox' and 'sent items' folders and whether any prejudice to the client would result if only hard copy items are provided."

Relying on New Hampshire RPC 1.16(d), which is identical in pertinent part to Model Rule 1.16(d) (a lawyer must "take steps to the extent reasonably practicable to protect a client's interests," such as "surrendering papers and property to which the client is entitled"), the New Hampshire Ethics Committee explained that (1) the contents of a client's file belong to the client; (2) upon request, an attorney must provide the file to the client;[63] (3) a client's file includes both paper and electronic documents and communications;[64] and (4) the "the mere existence of a paper file does not necessarily allow a firm to automatically exclude from the client's file electronic communications and other computer-based writings."[65]

---

made to contact the client and deliver the documents to him or her. Documents which fall into category 4 could be appropriately destroyed."

[62] Http://www.nhbar.org/uploads/pdf/Opinion2005-06-03.pdf.

[63] The New Hampshire Ethics Committee cited a New Hampshire decision, Averill v. Cox, 145 N.H. 328, 339 (2000), for propositions (1) and (2).

[64] ABA Model Rule 1.0 defines "writing" as "a tangible or electronic record of a communication or representation, including handwriting, typewriting, printing, photostating, photography, audio or videorecording, and e-mail." The Model Rules reflect that with increased reliance on electronic communications and records in the practice of law, it is reasonable to assume that a client's file can include electronic communications, such as e-mails, as well as electronic versions of documents filed on behalf of a client.

[65] In concluding that a client's file includes electronic documents, the New Hampshire Ethics Committee relied in part on the definition of "writing" in Model Rule 1.0. At the time

The committee then concluded that despite the burden, the law firm had the obligation to provide the files, suggesting that word searches could be used to manage the burden and that the law firm had to avoid releasing information that "might harm a third party":

> Therefore, if a client requests a copy of her file, the firm has an obligation to provide all files pertinent to representation of that client, regardless of the burden that it might impose upon the firm to do so. See Averill at 339-40. That burden can be managed, in any event, through computer word search functions or other means that are routinely used for discovery or other purposes. As in discovery-related matters, it is incumbent upon the firm to manage its electronic and other files in a way that will allow for release of a file to a client without releasing other information that might harm a third party.[66]

The committee also cautioned the law firm to "take into account whether it has adequately notified this or other former clients of any file destruction policies followed by the firm with regard to both electronic and paper files."

The Illinois State Bar Association (ISBA), in its Advisory Opinion 01-01 (2001),[67] also determined that a client's file includes electronic, and not just paper, forms of documents or communications. Once again, a lawyer ("Attorney Jones") left the "ABC" law firm and the clients of Attorney Jones asked ABC to transfer their files, "including any generated, stored or archived on computer" to Attorney Jones. ABC sent hard

---

of the opinion, New Hampshire had not adopted Model Rule 1.0. That was remedied on January 1, 2008, when New Hampshire adopted revised rules of professional conduct. *See* http://www.courts.state.nh.us/rules/pcon/index.htm.

[66] Key word searches and the last admonition presumably were mentioned because the law firm did not have a document management system in place. If the law firm had a document management system in place that allowed files to be identified by the creator or editor of a document and by client name and matter, then, presumably, the burden of retrieval and production—while potentially time-consuming depending upon the number of clients and number of files—should be manageable. Producing the departing lawyer's e-mails should not have been that difficult assuming that e-mails of the departing lawyer were stored in files unique to the departing lawyer. The opinion does not discuss whether e-mails were located on backup tapes. Nor does it discuss whether the e-mails of the departing lawyer contained information relating to clients of the law firm that were staying with the law firm. If they did, the review, segregation, and production burden on the law firm would be greater.

[67] Illinois ethics opinions are available online to members of the Illinois Bar. *See* http://www.illinoisbar.org/resources/ethics/index.html. The text of the opinion appears in Appendix IV.

copies of documents in the client files to Attorney Jones. ABC did not search its computer system for client materials, "nor did the firm undertake any comparison of documents on computer with the file materials put in boxes and sent over to Attorney Jones."

The law firm invited Attorney Jones to go through the boxes to see whether any documents were missing. It would then "make an attempt to search the firm's computer to see about the whereabouts of those particular documents." In response, Attorney Jones "requested that the ABC law firm merely download onto disk(s) all the client(s) file materials and then Attorney Jones would compare what is on the disk(s) to what is contained in the boxes."

One other fact was important. "To download client file materials is easy to accomplish and client file materials on computer are accessed by attorney ID number, attorney initials and/or client name." Nonetheless, the "ABC law firm refuses to turn over client materials on computer to date." Was it correct in so refusing?

The ISBA Ethics Committee decided it was not. Citing what was then the Illinois equivalent to Model Rules 1.4(c)(4) and Model Rules 1.6(a) and 1.15(b), the committee determined that a client is entitled to access to its files, but acknowledged that the rules of professional conduct do not speak to the format of the production. Using the Illinois rules of civil procedure as guidance, the committee reasoned as follows:

(1) Under Illinois R. Civ. P. 201(b)(1), "documents" include "all retrievable information in computer storage" and, based on rules committee comments, a party is obligated to "produce on paper those relevant materials which have been stored electronically";

(2) Again citing rules committee comments, under Illinois R. Civ. P. 214, a party must include in that party's production response "all responsive information in computer storage in printed form" and "that there can be no question but that a producing party must search its computer storage when responding to a request to produce documents pursuant to this rule"; and

(3) "While discovery rules do not control issues of professional conduct, both sets of rules are promulgated by the Illinois Supreme Court, and should therefore be interpreted in a consistent manner."

As a result, the ISBA ethics committee concluded that on the facts presented,

> [T]he ABC law firm must download Attorney Jones's client file materials onto disks. It is also the Committee's opinion that the request to have client file materials downloaded onto disk is a "reasonable" request as set forth in Rule 1.4(a), and that the client is entitled to receive his or her files in the format in which the lawyer or law firm maintains such files.

As noted earlier, downloading was "easy to accomplish" because of the ABC law firm's electronic filing system. That prompted the committee to add, "it would be far more efficient and cost-effective" to require downloading by the law firm "than to require Attorney Jones to search through the boxes in order to figure out what documents may be missing."[68]

---

[68] The ISBA ethics committee suggested that the ABC law firm may be able to recover the reasonable expenses incurred to retrieve the electronic files: "Although the expense which would be incurred in downloading the client file materials is likely to be minimal, as set forth in ISBA Opinion No. 94-14, the ABC law firm may be entitled to compensation for the reasonable expense involved in retrieving the files in question and providing on disk copies of materials that were already provided to Attorney Jones and his clients." ISBA Opinion No. 94-14 appears in Appendix IV. It addressed the return of client files and the allocation of costs associated with the return. The ISBA ethics committee determined that: (1) Original papers delivered to the lawyer by the client had to be returned to the client, but the lawyer was entitled to make copies of this material at the lawyer's expense; (2) "With respect to other parts of the lawyer's file to which the client is entitled to access, including copies of documents that the client has already received, the originals may be retained by the lawyer and the client should be permitted to have copies at the client's expense;" (3) It did not "believe that a lawyer is required to act as a storage facility for clients, and therefore the lawyer is entitled to compensation for the reasonable expense involved in retrieving the files in question and providing copies of materials that the client has already received;" (4) "The lawyer is also entitled to compensation for the reasonable expense of providing copies of any materials, such as routine administrative correspondence with third parties, that the client may not have received because the lawyer had no duty to provide the client with copies of such materials in the normal course of the representation, but to which the client is entitled to access upon reasonable request;" and (5) The lawyer "may charge the reasonable expense of locating and copying those parts of the lawyer's file that the client has not provided, but to which the client is entitled to access" (since the lawyer's duty of confidentiality to other clients would preclude the client from direct access to files that contain other client information). Presumably the reference to ISBA Opinion No. 94-14 was intended to mean that the cost of retrieving electronically stored information could be shifted to the client where the lawyer had no duty to provide the client with such materials in the normal course of representation, the lawyer had already provided the client with electronic copies during the course of the representation, or the lawyer had to access files that contained information about other clients which would preclude direct access by the departing client.

Confidentiality concerns prompted by Model Rule 1.6(a) were also not a concern, according to the ISBA Ethics Committee, because of the filing system of the law firm.

> While it is certainly true that there would be information on the law firm's other client files stored on the computer that would constitute a confidence or secret of the other clients, the fact inquiry states that client file materials on the ABC law firm's computer are accessed by attorney i.d. number, attorney initials and/or client name. Accordingly, the ABC law firm could download only Attorney Jones's client files without fear of disclosing the confidences of its other clients.

The State Bar of California Standing Committee on Professional Responsibility and Conduct (COPRAC), in its Formal Opinion No. 2007-174,[69] addressed the ethical obligations of a lawyer who is replaced by a client in the middle of representation on both transactional and litigation work. The client asked the terminated lawyer for electronic versions of pleadings, discovery requests, and discovery responses in a pending lawsuit. The client also sought the electronic deposition and exhibit database, as well as transactional documents in another matter, to provide to new counsel. The client asked for all e-mail communications in both matters in electronic format "for ease of searching."

The terminated lawyer refused to release these items, "claiming that each contains metadata reflecting confidential information belonging to other clients." The COPRAC noted that the lawyer did not make any work product claims.

Under California's RPC 3-700(D), a lawyer is required to release "all client papers and property" upon termination of employment. "Client papers and property" include "correspondence, pleadings, deposition transcripts, exhibits, physical evidence, expert's reports, and other items reasonably necessary to the client's representation, whether the client has paid for them or not . . . ."[70] Emphasizing that Rule 3-700(D) refers to

---

[69] Http://www.calbar.ca.gov/calbar/pdfs/ethics/2007-174.pdf.

[70] Http://www.calbar.ca.gov/state/calbar/calbar_generic.jsp?sImagePath=Current_Rules.gif&sCategoryPath=/Home/Attorney%20Resources/Rules%20%26%20Regulations/Rules%20of%20Professional%20Conduct&sFileType=HTML&sCatHtmlPath=html/RPC_Current-Rules-3-700.html. The COPRAC further explained that the attorney must make "such release of client papers and property at no cost to the client." COPRAC Formal Op. 2007-174, at 2. The attorney may, however, enter into an agreement that provides that the client will pay for the cost of making a copy of the papers and property for the attorney to retain. *Id.* at n.3.

"all" client papers and property, the COPRAC determined that the term encompasses electronic papers and property. COPRAC Formal Opinion 2007-174, p. 3.

The COPRAC then explained that the correspondence and pleadings were expressly covered by Rule 3-700(D) and that deposition and exhibit databases came "within the listed categories of 'deposition transcripts,' and 'exhibits.'" With respect to discovery requests and responses, and transactional documents, the COPRAC acknowledged that the description of "client papers and property" does not list these items, but determined that they are embraced by the term, "other items reasonably necessary to the client's representation."

> An item is "reasonably necessary to the client's representation" if it is "generated during the representation" for continuing use therein. Discovery requests and responses satisfy this definition, since they may give rise to further discovery requests and responses and may also be included as exhibits to motions and as exhibits at trial. Transactional documents satisfy this definition as well, since they are used for purposes including monitoring performance under the original agreement underlying the transaction in question and any related agreement between the parties to that transaction and third parties who subsequently become involved.

COPRAC Formal Opinion 2007-174, p. 3-4 (emphasis in original, footnote omitted). Since the form of the client's papers and property is immaterial, the COPRAC advised that the terminated lawyer was obliged to release to the client the electronic versions of the requested e-mails, pleadings, discovery requests and responses, deposition and exhibit databases, and transactional documents. *Id.*, p. 4.[71]

The COPRAC did draw the line on the issue of software applications:

> The Committee also believes that whenever an attorney is obligated by rule 3-700(D)(1) to release items in electronic form, the attorney is not obligated to release them in any application (e.g., Word (.doc) or WordPerfect (.wpd)) other than the application in which the attorney possesses them. That is because the attorney's

[71] The COPRAC specifically rejected a "balancing test" weighing the need for the electronic versions against the time and money required for the attorney to copy and transfer the data. It also explained that the attorney could avoid substantial expense by employing "one of many commonly available electronic filing systems." COPRAC Formal Op. 2007-174, at 4.

> obligation is to release items, not to create them or to change the application.

COPRAC Formal Opinion 2007-174, p. 4 (emphasis in original, footnote omitted).

And what of the claim of confidential metadata? The COPRAC did not appear sympathetic, explaining that the lawyer had to strip the metadata prior to release of the electronic papers and property:

> Attorney A's presumptive obligation under rule 3-700(D), however, must be considered in light of Attorney A's claim that each of the electronic items in question contains metadata reflecting confidential information belonging to other clients. That is because an attorney is obligated under subdivision (e)(1) of section 6068 of the Business and Professions Code to protect each client's confidential information. Under the compulsion of that obligation, Attorney A would have to take reasonable steps to strip any metadata reflecting confidential information belonging to other clients from any of the electronic items prior to releasing them to Client. Inasmuch as Attorney A has not invoked the attorney work product doctrine, that doctrine is not implicated on the facts presented.

COPRAC Formal Opinion 2007-174, p. 5 (footnote omitted).

Model Rules 5.1 and 5.2 and the Responsibilities of Partners and Subordinate Lawyers

Model Rule 5.1 provides:

> (a) A partner in a law firm, and a lawyer who individually or together with other lawyers possesses comparable managerial authority in a law firm, shall make reasonable efforts to ensure that the firm has in effect measures giving reasonable assurance that all lawyers in the firm conform to the Rules of Professional Conduct.
> (b) A lawyer having direct supervisory authority over another lawyer shall make reasonable efforts to ensure that the other lawyer conforms to the Rules of Professional Conduct.
> (c) A lawyer shall be responsible for another lawyer's violation of the Rules of Professional Conduct if:
> (1) the lawyer orders or, with knowledge of the specific conduct, ratifies the conduct involved; or
> (2) the lawyer is a partner or has comparable managerial authority in the law firm in which the other lawyer practices, or has direct supervisory authority over the other lawyer, and

> knows of the conduct at a time when its consequences can be avoided or mitigated but fails to take reasonable remedial action.

Model Rule 5.2 provides in full:

> (a) A lawyer is bound by the Rules of Professional Conduct notwithstanding that the lawyer acted at the direction of another person.
> (b) A subordinate lawyer does not violate the Rules of Professional Conduct if that lawyer acts in accordance with a supervisory lawyer's reasonable resolution of an arguable question of professional duty.

The message of these rules is not complicated. Lawyers must reasonably ensure that those whom they oversee are competent under Model Rule 1.1 and are otherwise in compliance with the applicable rules of professional conduct.

Similarly, lawyers who are overseen by others are still bound by the rules of professional conduct even if they are taking direction from another lawyer. In a case of the "blind leading the blind," the subordinate lawyer must speak up if the rules of professional conduct are not being followed by the supervisory lawyer.

Under Model Rule 5.1, there is an "actual knowledge" requirement to hold a supervisory lawyer responsible for the failure of a supervised lawyer to comply with the rules of professional conduct. However, lawyers must be aware of differences between Model Rule 5.1 and any variation adopted in a particular jurisdiction. Illustratively, the District of Columbia has a "knew or should have known" requirement. D.C. RPC 5.1(c)(2) provides in pertinent part that a lawyer "shall be responsible for another lawyer's violation of the Rules of Professional Conduct if":

> The lawyer has direct supervisory authority over the other lawyer or is a partner or has comparable managerial authority in the law firm or government agency in which the other lawyer practices, and knows or reasonably should know of the conduct at a time when its consequences can be avoided or mitigated but fails to take reasonable remedial action.

In re Cohen, 847 A.2d 1162 (D.C. 2004) illustrates the importance of this difference. An associate in a law firm withdrew a trademark application for a client, Dr. Schleicher, telling the Patent and Trademark Office that the client had "expressly abandoned its above-referenced trademark application." *Id.* at 1166. The statement was false. The client was not aware of the filing and had not endorsed it. The PTO accepted the abandonment of the application. The associate was supervised by Cohen. Disciplinary proceedings were instituted against Cohen. The D.C. Board of Professional Responsibility found Cohen to be in violation of, among others, D.C. Rule 5.1(c)(2). Cohen conceded that "there was no system in place to impart rudimentary ethics training to lawyers in the firm," and there was no "review mechanism which allowed an associate's work to be reviewed and guided by a supervisory attorney." But he argued that he should not be punished for professional misconduct where he had no actual knowledge of the associate's misrepresentation. *Id.* The D.C. Court of Appeals rejected the plea.

> Rule 5.1(c)(2) in this jurisdiction represents a judgment that attorneys supervising other lawyers must take reasonable steps to become knowledgeable about the actions of those attorneys in representing clients of the firm. As the Board explained, the "reasonably know" provision was carefully crafted to encourage—indeed to require—supervising attorneys to reasonably monitor the course of a representation such as respondent's firm had undertaken on behalf of Dr. Schleicher, denying them the ostrich-like excuse of saying, in effect, "I didn't know and didn't want to know."
>
> . . .
>
> In reaching this conclusion, the Board took into account a number of factors including the discreet nature of the case, the extended length of the representation, the small size of the firm, and of course, the degree of supervision or lack thereof. The Board stated:
>
> > "Therefore, in the particular circumstances of this case, we conclude that Bar Counsel has established a violation of Rule 5.1(c)(2) because respondent reasonably should have known of the withdrawal application and should have been able to take reasonable remedial action to avoid its consequences. We believe a lawyer of reasonable prudence and competence would have made the inquiry necessary to determine the status of the application proceeding."
>
> We adopt this conclusion given the circumstances of this case.

Id. at 1166-67. This case illustrates the importance to supervisory lawyers of knowing not only their jurisdiction's counterpart to Model Rule 5.1, but also what supervised lawyers are doing. In the e-discovery arena, competent supervision goes hand in hand with proper training and oversight.

Model Rule 5.3 and Responsibilities Regarding Nonlawyer Assistants

Model Rule 5.3 provides:

> With respect to a nonlawyer employed or retained by or associated with a lawyer:
>
> (a) a partner, and a lawyer who individually or together with other lawyers possesses comparable managerial authority in a law firm shall make reasonable efforts to ensure that the firm has in effect measures giving reasonable assurance that the person's conduct is compatible with the professional obligations of the lawyer;
> (b) a lawyer having direct supervisory authority over the nonlawyer shall make reasonable efforts to ensure that the person's conduct is compatible with the professional obligations of the lawyer; and
> (c) a lawyer shall be responsible for conduct of such a person that would be a violation of the Rules of Professional Conduct if engaged in by a lawyer if:
> (1) the lawyer orders or, with the knowledge of the specific conduct, ratifies the conduct involved; or
> (2) the lawyer is a partner or has comparable managerial authority in the law firm in which the person is employed, or has direct supervisory authority over the person, and knows of the conduct at a time when its consequences can be avoided or mitigated but fails to take reasonable remedial action.

Lawyers will want to avoid what happened in *United Medical Supply Co., Inc. v. United States*, 2007 U.S. Claims LEXIS 207 (Ct. Claims June 27, 2007), where the district court described this exchange between the lawyer (Chadwick) and the paralegal (Brown) in connection with a number of e-discovery miscues regarding documents located at "medical treatment facilities" (MTFs):

> In his affidavit, Mr. Brown claimed that he had mistakenly believed that Mr. Chadwick wanted information only from the "eight or fewer MTFs" that possessed responsive documents. Mr. Brown further stated that he "was not aware that the representations I made were going to be conveyed to the Court." In his affidavit, Mr. Chadwick stated that he was "positive Mr. Brown understood I would convey to opposing counsel and the Court his findings as to the existence and location of relevant documents," noting that "[t]here could essentially have been no other purpose for the document search." In addition, Mr. Chadwick further stated that he had advised Mr. Brown "that the Court had raised questions during one or more status conferences regarding the thoroughness of our search." Mr. Chadwick further asserted that he believed that Mr. Brown knew that he was supposed to be contacting all of the MTFs, noting, inter alia, that a July 18, 2005, e-mail he sent to Mr. Brown and others specifically referred to the need "to provide additional information and documents, and to round up witnesses, from [18] military treatment facilities across the Southwest U.S." Finally, Mr. Chadwick indicated that when, in the process of obtaining the affidavits required by the court's June 13, 2006, order, he learned that certain MTFs had not been asked to turn over documents, he sent an e-mail to Mr. Brown asking him to comment on the situation, to which Mr. Brown assertedly replied, "[m]y bad."

Id. at **15.

The buck also has to stop with the supervising lawyer when a third-party e-discovery vendor is being managed by the lawyer. *Cf. Mays v. Neal*, 938 S.W.2d 830, 835 (Ark. 1997) (invoking Mo. RPC 5.3(b) and saying: "while a lawyer may delegate certain tasks to his assistants, he or she, as supervising attorney, has the ultimate responsibility for compliance by the nonlawyer with the applicable provisions of the Model Rules"); and *In Re Flack*, 33 P.3d 1281, 1287 (Kan. 2001) (a lawyer who contracted with a probate services company violated Kansas RPC 5.3 "when he failed to properly supervise the client service representatives and when he failed to assure that the actions of the client service representatives were compatible with his professional obligations as a lawyer").

There is no question that a party is responsible for its e-discovery vendor's errors. See *In re Seroquel Products Liability Litigation*, 2007 U.S. Dist. LEXIS 61287, *49-50 (M.D. Fla. Aug. 21, 2007) (a party is responsible for the errors of its vendors, citing Sedona Principle 6.d: "Ultimate responsibility for ensuring the preservation, collection, processing, and production of electronically stored information rests with the party and its counsel, not with the nonparty consultant or vendor."). If a lawyer assumes the management of a third-party vendor, it will behoove the lawyer to know what else the Sedona Principles say about vendors, since courts often cite these principles in e-discovery matters:

> Due to the complexity of electronic discovery, many organizations rely on consultants to provide a variety of services, including discovery planning, data collection, specialized data processing, and forensic analysis. Such consultants can be of great assistance to parties and courts in providing technical expertise and experience with the collection, review, and production of electronically stored information. However, parties should carefully consider the experience and expertise of a potential consultant before his or her selection, as standards for experts and consultants in this field have not been fully developed. Vendors offer a variety of software and services to assist with the electronic discovery process and a party's evaluation of vendor software and services should include the defensibility of the process in the litigation context, the cost, and the experience of the vendor. Ultimate responsibility for ensuring the preservation, collection, processing, and production of electronically stored information rests with the party and its counsel, not with the nonparty consultant or vendor.
>
> At all times, counsel, clients, and vendors must understand everyone's role in the discovery process. Thus, even if a vendor is retained to serve in a non-testifying capacity, everyone should be aware of the potential need for testimony if forensic or other technical expertise is required to prepare electronically stored information for review or production. Additionally, care should be taken to ensure that the vendor does not assume the role of a legal advisor, and that all persons involved understand what communications are protected under the attorney-client privilege and what information may be protected as attorney work product.[72]

[72] Http://www.thesedonaconference.org/content/miscFiles/TSC_PRINCP_2nd_ed_607.pdf, at 40.

And before ending this chapter, I return to where I began: Rule 1.1. Lawyers must be mindful of both this rule, demanding competence, and Rule 5.3, before undertaking the responsibility to manage a third-party e-discovery vendor.[73]

[73] The dollars involved in dealing with e-discovery vendors can be large. To illustrate, Sullivan & Cromwell (S&C) sued a vendor for alleged mistakes in handling e-discovery issues. In a complaint filed December 28, 2007, in the Southern District of New York, S&C accused Electronic Evidence Discovery, Inc. (EED) of "untimely and inaccurate" work. S&C asked the district court to declare that it did not have to pay a $710,000 bill from EED. *See* http://www.law.com/jsp/article.jsp?id=1199441137204. EED responded by suing S&C in King County Superior Court in Washington on January 7, 2008, demanding payment of $660,016.17, plus interest in the amount of $58,592.07. The matter was quickly and confidentially settled according to a January 18, 2008, report in the *New York Law Journal*. Disputes can also arise where a vendor is terminated in the middle of litigation and raises cost demands before returning the client's electronically stored information. Vendors do make mistakes. PSEG Power New York Inc. v. Alberici Constructors, 2007 U.S. Dist. LEXIS 66767 (N.D.N.Y. Sept. 7, 2007) (vendor separated 3,000 e-mails from their attachments); *In re* Seroquel Products Liability Litigation, 2007 U.S. Dist. LEXIS 61287, *37-38 (M.D. Fla. Aug. 21, 2007) ("a significant portion of the production had blank pages; new load files were not searchable, in part because the date formats in the metadata were inconsistently loaded and email attachments not consistently associated or identified; authors were not identified as custodians for files; transposed metadata recipients/authors; and no page breaks were inserted in 3.75 million pages.")

CHAPTER FOUR

Qualcomm v. Broadcom

In *Qualcomm Inc. v. Broadcom Corp.*, 2008 WL 66932 (S.D. Calif. Jan. 7, 2008), the magistrate judge sanctioned six lawyers for the failure of their client to conduct a proper search for electronic documents. Qualcomm ultimately produced—after trial—46,000 documents representing more than 300,000 pages that were relevant to the issues in the litigation and that, according to Qualcomm's letter of apology to the district court, "revealed facts that appear to be inconsistent with certain arguments that [counsel] made on Qualcomm's behalf at trial and in the equitable hearing following trial." *Id.* at *6. The lawyers were referred to the California Bar for "an appropriate investigation and imposition of possible sanctions." *Id.* at *18. The six sanctioned lawyers were not permitted by the magistrate judge to use attorney-client privileged communications to defend themselves. *Id.* at *13. They appealed the magistrate's decision in this regard.

The district court agreed with the six sanctioned lawyers and vacated this portion of the magistrate's order to permit the lawyers to put on evidence, presumably about who was responsible for the failure to produce the electronically stored information during discovery. 2008 WL 638108, *3 (S.D. Calif. March 5, 2008). In words that should give no comfort to either the six sanctioned lawyers or the Qualcomm lawyers, whose actions, presumably, will be the focus of the sanctioned lawyers' defense, the district court told the magistrate judge that her discretion "regarding responsibility and sanctions, if any, are not limited, either upwardly or downwardly, by the Order of Remand." *Id.* at *2.

The Duty of Candor Under Model Rule 3.3 Trumps Confidentiality Under Model Rule 1.6

Qualcomm represents a colossal e-discovery failure. The magistrate judge noted several provisions of the California RPC that may have been violated.

> If Mammen and Batchelder were unable to get Qualcomm to conduct a competent and thorough document search, they should have withdrawn from the case or taken other action to ensure production of the evidence. *See* The State Bar of California, Rules of Professional Conduct, Rule 5-220 (a lawyer shall not suppress evidence that the lawyer or the lawyer's client has a legal obligation to reveal); Rule 3-700 (a lawyer shall withdraw from employment if the lawyer knows or should know that continued employment will result in a violation of these rules or the client insists that the lawyer pursue a course of conduct prohibited under these rules). Attorneys' ethical obligations do not permit them to participate in an inadequate document search and then provide misleading and incomplete information to their opponents and false arguments to the court. *Id.*; Rule 5-200 (a lawyer shall not seek to mislead the judge or jury by a false statement of fact or law); *see also In re Marriage of Gong and Kwong*, 157 Cal. App. 4th 939, 951 (1st Dist. 2007) ("[a]n attorney in a civil case is not a hired gun required to carry out every direction given by the client;" he must act like the professional he is).

The analogous Model Rules are Model Rules 3.4(a)(1) and 1.16(a), both discussed above, as well as Model Rule 3.3, which has not yet been mentioned. For ease of reference, again, Model Rule 3.4(a) provides:

> A lawyer shall not:
>
> (a) unlawfully obstruct another party's access to evidence or unlawfully alter, destroy or conceal a document or other material having potential evidentiary value. A lawyer shall not counsel or assist another person to do any such act; . . .

Model Rule 1.16(a)(1) provides:

> (a) Except as stated in paragraph (c), a lawyer shall not represent a client or, where representation has commenced, shall withdraw from the representation of a client if:
>
> > (1) the representation will result in violation of the Rules of Professional Conduct or other law; . . .

Finally, Model Rule 3.3(a)(1) and (3) are part of the duty of candor that every lawyer owes to a court. They provide:

> (a) A lawyer shall not knowingly:
>
> (1) make a false statement of fact or law to a tribunal or fail to correct a false statement of material fact or law previously made to the tribunal by the lawyer; . . .
>
> (3) offer evidence that the lawyer knows to be false. If a lawyer, the lawyer's client, or a witness called by the lawyer, has offered material evidence and the lawyer comes to know of its falsity, the lawyer shall take reasonable remedial measures, including, if necessary, disclosure to the tribunal. A lawyer may refuse to offer evidence, other than the testimony of a defendant in a criminal matter, that the lawyer reasonably believes is false.

As discussed earlier, Model Rule 1.6 requires lawyers to maintain the confidentiality of client information. Model Rule 1.6(b) does, however, permit disclosure "to the extent the lawyer reasonably believes necessary:"[1]

> (1) to prevent reasonably certain death or substantial bodily harm;
>
> (2) to prevent the client from committing a crime or fraud[2] that is reasonably certain to result in substantial injury to the financial interests or property of another and in furtherance of which the client has used or is using the lawyer's services;
>
> (3) to prevent, mitigate or rectify substantial injury to the financial interests or property of another that is reasonably certain to result or has resulted from the client's commission of a crime or fraud in furtherance of which the client has used the lawyer's services;
>
> (4) to secure legal advice about the lawyer's compliance with these Rules;

[1] Comment [14] (2003) gives content to this phrase. "Where practicable, the lawyer should first seek to persuade the client to take suitable action to obviate the need for disclosure. In any case, a disclosure adverse to the client's interest should be no greater than the lawyer reasonably believes necessary to accomplish the purpose. If the disclosure will be made in connection with a judicial proceeding, the disclosure should be made in a manner that limits access to the information to the tribunal or other persons having a need to know it and appropriate protective orders or other arrangements should be sought by the lawyer to the fullest extent practicable."

[2] As a reminder, Model Rule 1.0(d) defines "fraud": "'Fraud' or 'fraudulent' denotes conduct that is fraudulent under the substantive or procedural law of the applicable jurisdiction and has a purpose to deceive."

> (5) to establish a claim or a defense in a controversy between the lawyer and the client, to establish a defense in a criminal or civil claim against the lawyer based upon conduct in which the client was involved, or to respond to allegations in any proceeding concerning the lawyer's representation of the client; or
> (6) to comply with other law or court order.

Model Rule 1.6(b)(5) codifies the common law right of a lawyer to use privileged information where necessary to establish a defense where there is "controversy" between the client and the lawyer. Had *Qualcomm* arisen in a model-rule jurisdiction, the lawyers accused of discovery misconduct should have been able to invoke Model Rule 1.6(b)(5) in the initial sanctions hearing before the magistrate judge.[3]

That is hardly comforting, of course. The thought of a sanctions hearing at which in-house counsel and outside counsel are pointing fingers to establish each other's culpability should terrify all in-house counsel and their outside litigation counsel. If *Qualcomm* does not result in early and frequent collaboration, as well as constant communication between in-house counsel and their litigation counsel on e-discovery, the magistrate judge's final words will, indeed, have fallen on deaf ears:

[3] The district court in *Qualcomm* explained that declarations filed by Qualcomm employees were "exonerative of Qualcomm and critical of the services and advice of their retained counsel. None were filed under seal." As a result of this "introduction of accusatory adversity between Qualcomm and its retained counsel regarding the issue of assessing responsibility for the failure of discovery" the factual basis "which supported the court's earlier order denying the self-defense exception to Qualcomm's attorney-client privilege" was changed. 2008 WL 638108 at *3 (*citing* Meyerhofer v. Empire Fire & Marine Ins. Co., 497 F.2d 1190, 1194-95 (2d Cir.1974); Hearn v. Rhay, 68 F.R.D. 574, 581 (E.D. Wash. 1975); First Fed. Sav. & Loan Ass'n v. Oppenheim, Appel, Dixon & Co., 110 F.R.D. 557, 560-68 (S.D.N.Y. 1986); ABA MODEL RULES OF PROF'L CONDUCT R. 1.6(b)(5) & cmt. 10). Comment [10] to Model Rule 1.6(b) provides in pertinent part that, "Where a legal claim or disciplinary charge alleges complicity of the lawyer in a client's conduct or other misconduct of the lawyer involving representation of the client, the lawyer may respond to the extent the lawyer reasonably believes necessary to establish a defense .... The lawyer's right to respond arises when an assertion of such complicity has been made. Paragraph (b)(5) does not require the lawyer to await the commencement of an action or proceeding that charges such complicity, so that the defense may be established by responding directly to a third party who has made such an assertion. The right to defend also applies, of course, where a proceeding has been commenced." The district court in *Qualcomm* concluded that, "The attorneys have a due process right to defend themselves under the totality of circumstances presented in this sanctions hearing where their alleged conduct regarding discovery is in conflict with that alleged by Qualcomm concerning performance of discovery responsibilities. *See, e.g.,* Miranda v. So. Pac. Transp. Co., 710 F.2d 516, 522-23 (9th Cir. 1983)." 2008 WL 638108, at *3.

> While no one can undo the misconduct in this case, this process,[4] hopefully, will establish a baseline for other cases. Perhaps it also will establish a turning point in what the Court perceives as a decline in and deterioration of civility, professionalism and ethical conduct in the litigation arena. To the extent it does so, everyone benefits—Broadcom, Qualcomm, and all attorneys who engage in, and judges who preside over, complex litigation. If nothing else, it will provide a road map to assist counsel and corporate clients in complying with their ethical and discovery obligations and conducting the requisite "reasonable inquiry."

2008 WL 66932, at *20.

Had Qualcomm's outside counsel[5] known of the failure to produce documents, they would have had to honor their certification and investigative obligations under Fed. R. Civ. P. 26(g)[6] and their supplementation

---

[4] The magistrate judge was referring to a protocol she required the Qualcomm attorneys and the six sanctioned attorneys to prepare. She called it the "Comprehensive Case Review and Enforcement of Discovery Obligations" or "CREDO" program. It was to contain a "detailed analysis" of what went wrong, how to fix what went wrong, and how to ensure that a similar e-discovery failure would not occur, not just at Qualcomm but at other organizations facing e-discovery obligations. 2008 WL 66932, at *19.

[5] I assume in this analysis that in-house counsel have not appeared as counsel of record or as signatories to any discovery responses.

[6] Fed. R. Civ. P. 26(g)(1) addresses initial disclosures under Fed. R. Civ. P. 26(a) and states: "Every disclosure under Rule 26(a)(1) or (a)(3) and every discovery request, response, or objection must be signed by at least one attorney of record in the attorney's own name . . . . By signing, an attorney or party certifies that to the best of the person's knowledge, information, and belief formed after a reasonable inquiry: (A) with respect to a disclosure, it is complete and correct as of the time it is made; and (B) with respect to a discovery request, response, or objection, it is: (i) consistent with these rules and warranted by existing law or by a nonfrivolous argument for extending, modifying, or reversing existing law, or for establishing new law; (ii) not interposed for any improper purpose, such as to harass, cause unnecessary delay, or needlessly increase the cost of litigation; and (iii) neither unreasonable nor unduly burdensome or expensive, considering the needs of the case, prior discovery in the case, the amount in controversy, and the importance of the issues at stake in the action." The district court in Cache La Poudre Feeds, LLC v. Land O'Lakes, Inc., et al., 2007 U.S. Dist. LEXIS 15277, *40-41 (D. Colo. Mar. 2, 2007), explained that an attorney is entitled to rely on the assertions of the client under Fed. R. Civ. P. 26(g) provided that "'the investigation undertaken by the attorney *and the conclusions drawn therefrom* are reasonable under the circumstances.' Advisory Committee Notes to the 1983 Amendments to Fed.R.Civ.P. 26(g). *But [see] also* Metropolitan Opera Ass'n, Inc. v. Local 100 Hotel Employees and Restaurant Employees International Union, 212 F.R.D. 178, 221-224 (S.D.N.Y. 2003) (holding that defense counsel failed to comply with Fed. R. Civ. P. 26(g) by, *inter alia,* never adequately instructing defendant as to its overall discovery obligations, by failing

obligations under Fed. R. Civ. P. 26(e)(1)[7] before there would have been any consideration of their confidentiality obligations under Model Rule 1.6. And even if they could have somehow avoided their obligations under Fed. R. Civ. P. 26(g), the duty of candor under Model Rule 3.3 applies "even if compliance requires disclosure of information otherwise protected by Rule 1.6." Model Rule 3.3(c). In other words, the duty of candor to a tribunal trumps the duty of confidentiality.[8]

Whatever the magistrate judge in *Qualcomm* concludes on remand, no lawyer should ever permit his or her candor or honesty to be questioned, and certainly no lawyer should ever be associated with the presentation

---

to inquire about the client's document storage procedures and capabilities, by failing to implement a systematic procedure for document production or retention, and by failing to ask important witnesses for documents), *adhered to on reconsideration*, 2004 U.S. Dist. LEXIS 17093, 2004 WL 1943099."

[7] Fed. R. Civ. P. 26(e)(1)(A) provides that a party who has made an initial disclosure under Fed. R. Civ. P. 26(a) or responded to a request for production "must supplement or correct its disclosure or response: (A) in a timely manner if the party learns that in some material respect the disclosure or response is incomplete or incorrect, and if the additional or corrective information has not otherwise been made known to the other parties during the discovery process or in writing."

[8] *Cf.* Ohio's Rule 1.6(c) ("A lawyer shall reveal information relating to the representation of a client, including information protected by the attorney-client privilege under applicable law, to the extent the lawyer reasonably believes necessary to comply with Rule 3.3 or 4.1.") *See* Cleveland Hair Clinic, Inc. v. Puig, 200 F.3d 1063, 1067 (7th Cir. 2000) ("The duty to protect confidentiality does not come before the duty to be honest with the court."), and cases cited therein. *See also* ABA Formal Op. 93-376 (August 6, 1993) (duty of candor applies where a witness lied in a deposition taken during discovery: "The Committee is therefore of the view that, in the pretrial situation described above, the lawyer's duty of candor toward the tribunal under Rule 3.3 qualifies her duty to keep client confidences under Rule 1.6"). *See also* Rhode Island Ethics Advisory Panel Opinion 2007-6 (March 26, 2007). A lawyer had successfully represented a Social Security beneficiary before an administrative law judge (ALJ) on a claim for additional benefits. The client received a lump sum payment from the Social Security Administration for $12,000 more than the client was entitled to receive. The lawyer advised the client to return the money but it had already been spent, the lawyer was told. As a fee, the lawyer is entitled to 25 percent of the additional benefits. This amount is withheld from the benefit payment by the SSA until the lawyer files a fee request. Before filing the request, the lawyer sought ethical guidance since the fee being withheld was based on 25 percent of the incorrectly calculated benefits. The panel determined that the proceeding had not yet concluded since a fee petition still had to be made, and thus the attorney's duty of candor required the attorney to advise the ALJ of the error if the client refuses to notify the SSA of the error. "Insofar as the inquiring attorney must file a fee petition with the ALJ in order to receive his/her fee, the proceeding in this inquiry is not concluded. Therefore Rule 3.3, and not Rule 1.6, governs the conduct of the inquiring attorney." The attorney must also file a fee petition based on the correctly calculated benefit, the panel said. Http://www.courts.state.ri.us/supreme/ethics/ethicsopinions2007.htm.

of false information to a court. One should not need rules of professional conduct to understand these principles.

But what of in-house counsel who have not appeared as counsel of record? Do they have disclosure obligations? This intersection between e-discovery and ethics requires a lengthier explanation.

The Duty of Disclosure Imposed on In-House Counsel Under Model Rule 1.13

Model Rule 1.13(b)[9] addresses the "organization" as a client. It provides that if a lawyer "for an organization":[10]

> knows that an officer, employee or other person associated with the organization is engaged in action, intends to act or refuses to act in a matter related to the representation that is a violation of a legal obligation to the organization, or a violation of law which reasonably might be imputed to the organization, and that is likely to result in substantial injury to the organization, then the lawyer shall proceed as is reasonably necessary in the best interest of the organization. Unless the lawyer reasonably believes that it is not necessary in the best interest of the organization to do so, the lawyer shall refer the matter to higher authority in the organization, including, if warranted by the circumstances, the highest authority that can act on behalf of the organization as determined by applicable law.

Three aspects of the rule quickly attract a reader's attention. First, actual knowledge is required. Second, the operative language describes present or future conduct ("is engaged," "intends to act," "refuses to act") and not past conduct. Hence, immediately the applicability of this rule to a past act is questionable.[11] Third, Rule 1.13(b) is prescriptive ("shall

---

[9] California does not follow the Model Rules (one of two states that does not once New York adopts the Model Rules). Hence, this analysis may not be applicable under California's ethics rules.

[10] Rule 1.13(a) refers to a "lawyer employed or retained by an organization." Hence, Rule 1.13(b) covers both in-house and outside counsel. But in this e-discovery context, I address only in-house counsel.

[11] Comment [4] may be contemplating past acts, when it says: "Even in circumstances where a lawyer is not obligated to proceed by Rule 1.13, a lawyer may bring to the attention of an organizational client, including its highest authority, matters that the lawyer reasonably believes to be of sufficient importance to warrant doing so in the best interest of the organization." For past acts, Rule 1.6(b)(3) may be applicable but only if the lawyer's services were used in furtherance of a client's commission of a crime or fraud. If this

proceed" and "shall refer"), although this requirement is mildly limited by the phrases "as is reasonably necessary in the best interest of the organization," or "[u]nless the lawyer reasonably believes it is not necessary in the best interest of the organization to do so."

What is a violation of a legal obligation to the organization? Presumably it covers acts that would be characterized as not in the best interests of the organization. One should conclude that the failure to honor the corporation's discovery obligations in litigation falls into this category.

There is also a need for "substantial injury" to the organization. An intentional misstatement of expenses on an expense voucher would represent a violation of a legal obligation to the organization, but it might not result in "substantial injury." On the other hand, one must assume that violation of discovery obligations in litigation is "likely to result in substantial injury to the organization."[12] And a criminal law violation imputed to the organization would comfortably fall into this category.

Assuming a legal obligation to the organization is being violated and the "likely to result in substantial injury" standard is met, a lawyer for an organization then knows that he or she has to proceed "as is reasonably necessary in the best interest of the organization." What does that mean? Comment [3] to Rule 1.1.3 provides this guidance:

> When constituents of the organization make decisions for it, the decisions ordinarily must be accepted by the lawyer even if their utility or prudence is doubtful. Decisions concerning policy and operations, including ones entailing serious risk, are not as such in the lawyer's province. Paragraph (b) makes clear, however, that when the lawyer knows that the organization is likely to be substantially injured by action of an officer or other constituent that violates a legal obligation to the organization or is in violation of law that might be imputed to the organization, the lawyer must proceed as is reasonably necessary in the best interest of the organization. As defined in Rule 1.0(f), knowledge can be inferred from circumstances, and a lawyer cannot ignore the obvious. As defined

threshold is met, it would seem logical for a lawyer "for an organization" then to follow Rule 1.13 to make a Rule 1.6(b)(3) disclosure.

[12] A failure to produce 46,000 documents representing 300,000 pages of responsive information that contradicts positions taken before the district court and jury would unquestionably fall into the category of "likely to result in substantial injury to the organization." However, not every e-discovery search or production failure will fall into this category. Each situation would have to be judged on its unique facts.

> in Rule 1.0(f), knowledge can be inferred from circumstances, and a lawyer cannot ignore the obvious.

Comment [4] contains additional guidance:

> In determining how to proceed under Paragraph (b), the lawyer should give due consideration to the seriousness of the violation and its consequences, the responsibility in the organization and the apparent motivation of the person involved, the policies of the organization concerning such matters, and any other relevant considerations.

And what is an organization's lawyer armed with "knowledge" under Model Rule 1.13(b) then supposed to do? Rule 1.13(b) says the lawyer should refer the matter up the authority ladder:

> Unless the lawyer reasonably believes that it is not necessary in the best interest of the organization to do so, the lawyer shall refer the matter to higher authority in the organization, including, if warranted by the circumstances, the highest authority that can act on behalf of the organization as determined by applicable law.

With respect to an in-house counsel in a Model Rule 1.13 analysis, the less senior the in-house lawyer, the more likely it is that the general counsel or assistant general counsel would be the appropriate recipient of the referral. The more senior the in-house lawyer, the more likely it is that the referral would be made to a senior officer or, depending on the facts, one or more members of the board of directors.[13]

---

[13] Philadelphia Bar Association, Ethics Opinion 2006-7 (January 2007) addressed reporting under Rule 1.13 by outside counsel. The lawyer making the inquiry was former counsel to an organization that had applied for tax exempt status and then later decided to convert to a for-profit venture, without disclosing this fact to members and volunteers. The inquirer sought to determine whether the inquirer could disclose this fact to the members and volunteers but was told that, under Pa. Rules of Prof'l Conduct 1.13(a) and (b), disclosure should be made in writing to the board of directors that the inquirer was no longer counsel and the organization was at risk of being in violation of substantive law. The ethics committee appeared to assume the inquirer was still counsel to the organization even though the inquirer had advised the Internal Revenue Service of her disassociation as counsel. Http://www.philadelphiabar.org/page/EthicsOpinion2006-7?appNum=1&wosid=9rloAixh2jjM9dSViI9zA0.

Referral is Rule 1.13's preference. Comment [4] explains, "Ordinarily, referral to a higher authority would be necessary." However, Comment [4] also suggests giving the offending "constituent"[14] the opportunity to cure:

> In some circumstances, it may be appropriate for the lawyer to ask the constituent to reconsider the matter, for example, if the circumstances involve a constituent's innocent misunderstanding of law and subsequent acceptance of the lawyer's advice, the lawyer may reasonably conclude that the best interest of the organization does not require that the matter be referred to higher authority.[15]

In other words, if a junior lawyer on an in-house e-discovery team believes there have been e-discovery failures, the junior lawyer can first go to the person responsible on the team to "cure" the failures. The graver the failures, however, the more likely it is that communication with the offending constituent(s) will be preempted by direct contact with a higher authority. Comment [4] to Rule 1.13 agrees:

> If the matter is of sufficient seriousness and importance or urgency to the organization, referral to higher authority in the organization may be necessary even if the lawyer has not communicated with the constituent.

Suppose that the reporting lawyer has referred the matter to the general counsel and nothing happens. Should the lawyer go higher up the chain of command? Depending on the circumstances, it appears that the lawyer may have the obligation to go over the general counsel, since 1.13(b) provides for referral to a "higher" authority (say, the general counsel) but also allows for referral to the "highest" authority if "warranted by the circumstances."

However, in an in-house setting, another way to read Model Rule 1.13(b)(3) is to say that the less senior lawyer has satisfied his or her obligations by referral to a more senior lawyer who then has to consider his or her ethical obligations under Model Rule 1.13(b). Only when the

[14] A "constituent" would be an officer, director, employee, or shareholder. Rule 1.13, cmt. [1].

[15] If the constituent rejects this opportunity to cure, "it will be necessary for the lawyer to take steps to have the matter reviewed by a higher authority in the organization."

highest ranking in-house lawyer in the chain of command gets the problem does it then go to management, including, depending on the seriousness of the matter, the board of directors.[16]

Whether it is the first reporting lawyer or a reporting lawyer with higher authority, Rule 1.13(b) requires that the "matter" ultimately reach the "highest authority" that can act on behalf of the organization "as determined by applicable law."[17]

What is the remedy should the highest authority fail to act? Model Rule 1.13(c) provides that "except as provided in Paragraph (d),"[18] if

> (1) despite the lawyer's efforts in accordance with Paragraph (b) the highest authority that can act on behalf of the organization insists upon or fails to address in a timely and appropriate fashion action, or a refusal to act, that is clearly a violation of law, and
> (2) the lawyer reasonably believes that the violation is reasonably certain to result in substantial injury to the organization, then the lawyer may reveal information relating to the representation whether or not Rule 1.6 permits such disclosure, but only if and to the extent the lawyer reasonably believes necessary to prevent substantial injury to the organization.

Different thresholds apply when going outside the organization with a disclosure under Model Rule 1.13(c), than those that apply when making an up-the-ladder report within the organization under Rule 1.13(b). To make a Rule 1.13(b) report, a mixed standard is applied. A lawyer who knows "facts from which a reasonable lawyer, under the circumstances, would conclude" that an action is likely to result in substantial injury to the organization (an objective standard) is supposed to proceed "as is reasonably necessary in the best interest of the organization." Only when the lawyer reasonably believes it is not necessary (a subjective

[16] Comment [4] cautions the reporting lawyer to seek to maintain confidentiality within the organization: "Any measures taken should, to the extent practicable, minimize the risk of revealing information relating to the representation to persons outside the organization."
[17] Presumably, that will, in most cases, be the board of directors, as Comment [5] to Rule 1.13 states. Comment [5] recognizes that in certain circumstances, the independent directors of the corporation may be the appropriate recipients of a disclosure.
[18] Paragraph (d) provides: "Paragraph (c) shall not apply with respect to information relating to a lawyer's engagement by an organization to investigate an alleged violation of law, or to defend the organization or an officer, employee or other constituent associated with the organization against a claim arising out of an alleged violation of law."

standard),[19] is the lawyer supposed to refer the matter to higher authority in the organization. In contrast, to go outside the organization under Rule 1.13(c), there is a subjective standard ("the lawyer reasonably believes . . .").

Whereas Rule 1.13(b) requires a "violation of a legal obligation to the organization, or a violation of law which reasonably may be imputed to the organization," to go up the ladder, the ante is upped when going outside the organization—Rule 1.13(c) requires that the action or refusal to act is "clearly a violation of law."

In addition, to justify an up-the-ladder report, Rule 1.13(b) characterizes the act in question as one that "is *likely* to result in substantial injury to the organization." Under Rule 1.13(c), if the highest authority continues the conduct or fails to address the conduct in a timely and appropriate fashion, disclosure then requires that the "violation"—presumably referring to the violation of law in Rule 1.13(c)(1)—is *"reasonably certain* to result in substantial injury to the organization." The objective standard is tied to a likely result while the subjective standard is tied to a reasonably certain result.

Finally, Rule 1.13(b) uses prescriptive language ("shall proceed" and "shall refer") while Rule 1.13(c) uses permissive language ("may reveal").

Rule 1.13(c) does not identify the recipient of the information to be revealed. In a litigation context, one would presume that the in-house counsel would tell outside counsel there was a problem with the production, thereby triggering outside counsel's obligations to examine the discovery responses to ensure compliance with Fed. R. Civ. P. 26(e) and (g), as well as the duty of candor under Model Rule 3.3.

Note that under Rule 1.13, Rule 1.6 is not controlling.[20] The "lawyer employed or retained by an organization" under Rule 1.13(a) who gives the organization the opportunity to act through its highest authority may ignore Rule 1.6, but is limited to a disclosure that the lawyer reasonably believes (a subjective standard again) "necessary to prevent substantial injury to the organization." Unlike Rule 1.6, which requires that the lawyer's services be used in furtherance of the crime or fraud, Rule 1.13 is more expansive; it refers to "information relating to the representation"

[19] I call this a subjective standard because the lawyer decides what is a reasonable belief, in contrast to the earlier language in Model Rule 1.13(b), which makes reference to "facts from which a reasonable lawyer, under the circumstances, would conclude . . . ."

[20] Comment [6] explains that Paragraph (c) "supplements" Rule 1.6 but does "not modify, restrict, or limit" Rule 1.6's provisions.

or requires "that the matter be related to the lawyer's representation of an organization." Rule 1.13(c) and Comment [6].[21]

This is not the case in *Qualcomm*, but what happens if a reporting lawyer is discharged or withdraws before the highest authority in the organization learns of the lawyer's concerns?[22] May that lawyer still climb the reporting ladder to the highest authority or inform the highest authority of the discharge or withdrawal? Rule 1.13(e) gives the lawyer discretion on how to proceed:

> (e) A lawyer who reasonably believes that he or she has been discharged[23] because of the lawyer's actions taken pursuant to Paragraphs (b) or (c), or who withdraws in circumstances that require or permit the lawyer to take action under either of those Paragraphs,[24] shall proceed as the lawyer reasonably believes

---

[21] If the services of a lawyer for an organization are also being used in furtherance of a crime or fraud, Rule 1.6(b)(2) and (3) "may permit the lawyer to disclose confidential information." Rule 1.13, Comment [6]. If Rule 1.2(d) is applicable, "withdrawal from the representation under Rule 1.16(a)(1) may be required." *Id.* As discussed above, if the representation results in a violation of the rules of professional conduct, Rule 1.16 triggers mandatory withdrawal. Also, as discussed earlier, Rule 1.2(d) provides that a lawyer shall not counsel a client to engage, or assist a client, in conduct that the lawyer knows or reasonably knows is criminal or fraudulent. For an in-house counsel, presumably that means that the lawyer must resign.

[22] *Cf.* Formal Ethics Opinion 11, North Carolina Bar (January 18, 2001) (http://www.ncbar.com/ethics/ethics.asp?order=0) (Attorney A, employed by Corporation C, was assigned to monitor compliance with a settlement with the United States. Attorney A learns of a separate scheme to defraud the United States of $38 million through improper billings, involving the chief financial officer and chief executive officer of Corporation C. Attorney A informs the general counsel of the fraud scheme and, two weeks later, is fired. Attorney A has documents that reveal the scheme and wishes to approach the U.S. Attorney's office. The opinion provides that Attorney A may reveal confidential information if such information "concerns the intention of Corporation C to commit a crime and the information is necessary to prevent the crime." However, if the information relates to "past conduct, it may not be disclosed to the US Attorney." The opinion next states that confidential information may not be shared and recommended that in a wrongful termination action (permissible in North Carolina under the circumstances), Attorney A should obtain a ruling from the court on the scope of permitted disclosure after an *in camera* proffer of the confidential information).

[23] "Discharged" here presumably refers to an in-house counsel who has been terminated or an outside counsel that has been discharged.

[24] It is not clear what is meant by the phrase "circumstances that require or permit the lawyer to take action" under Rule 1.13(b) or (c) other than that the conditions of these paragraphs are satisfied.

necessary to assure that the organization's highest authority is informed of the lawyer's discharge or withdrawal.

Let's return to the in-house e-discovery undertaking.[25] Let's assume as is the case in *Qualcomm* that more than one lawyer is involved. Let's further assume that none of the in-house counsel has appeared as counsel of record or signed discovery responses. If other than the senior lawyer on the in-house team decides that the team has not performed an adequate search for documents—say because the team did not identify sufficient numbers of custodians, or it did but it did not adequately search storage media associated with the custodians, or, worse yet, that it did not search at all for certain categories of requested documents—under Model Rule 1.13(a), the lawyer should address the concern with the senior lawyer on the team or any other person who represents "higher authority in the organization, including, if warranted by the circumstances, the highest authority that can act on behalf of the organization as determined by applicable law." If the recipient of the info)rmation is a lawyer, then the recipient must decide how to proceed "as is reasonably necessary in the best interest of the organization" and may also have to refer the

[25] I assume in this analysis that the Sarbanes Oxley Act does not apply. In the case of a public company regulated by the Securities and Exchange Commission (SEC), Section 307 of the Sarbanes Oxley Act, 15 U.S.C. § 7245, required the SEC to adopt rules of professional conduct for lawyers "appearing and practicing" before it. To meet the requirements of Section 307, the SEC issued a final rule entitled, "Implementation of Standards of Professional Conduct for Attorneys." 17 C.F.R. Part 205 (issued on January 29, 2003, under the authority of Section 307 of the Sarbanes-Oxley Act of 2002, 68 Fed. Reg. 6296 (February 6, 2003), and adopted as a final rule effective August 5, 2003. Http://www.sec.gov/rules/final/33-8185.htm). Section 205.3(b) of the SEC's Standards of Professional Conduct provides for "up-the-ladder" reporting of "evidence of a material violation." A material violation is "a material violation of an applicable United States federal or state securities law, a material breach of fiduciary duty arising under United States federal or state law, or a similar material violation of any United States federal or state law." 17 CFR § 205.2(i). "Evidence of a material violation" means "credible evidence, based upon which it would be unreasonable, under the circumstances, for a prudent and competent attorney not to conclude that it is reasonably likely that a material violation has occurred, is ongoing, or is about to occur." 17 CFR § 205.2(e). A "breach of fiduciary duty" refers to any "breach of fiduciary duty or similar duty to the issuer recognized under an applicable Federal or State statute or at common law, including but not limited to misfeasance, nonfeasance, abdication of duty, abuse of trust, and approval of unlawful transactions." 17 C.F.R. § 205.2(d). *See generally*, Barkett, *Tattletales or Crimestoppers: Disclosure Ethics Under Model Rules 1.6 and 1.13*, presented at the ABA ANNUAL MEETING (Atlanta, August 7, 2004) and, in an updated version, at the ABA TORT AND INSURANCE PRACTICE SECTION SPRING CLE MEETING (Phoenix, April 11, 2008).

matter to higher authority or the highest authority depending upon the circumstances.

I will end the analysis here because I assume that no lawyer will want to be in the sequel to *Qualcomm.* In other words, appropriate remedial action will be taken within the organization working with outside counsel and, as appropriate, the district court.[26] However, if no action is taken to reverse the e-discovery misconduct, the lawyers who reported up the ladder will have to decide what actions to take under Model Rule 1.13(c).

Is there a simple conclusion to draw from this analysis? Taking any potential criminal conduct out of the discussion, it seems clear that an organization's lawyer who learns of civil conduct that has sufficiently large penalties attached to it has to move up the chain of command if the responsible constituent does not end the conduct.[27] Other conduct that represents a violation of a "legal obligation" to the organization or a violation of law that can be imputed to the organization must be likely to result in a "substantial injury" to the organization. If it does, the lawyer

---

[26] *See* United Medical Supply Co., Inc. v. United States, 2007 U.S. Claims LEXIS 207 (Ct. Claims June 27, 2007). The United States Department of Justice was responding to discovery requests in a matter involving discovery of documents located at medical treatment facilities (MTFs). DOJ counsel e-mailed a DOJ paralegal asking: "Peter, can you brief me on where we stand?" The paralegal responded: "Where we stand is that I don't know of anywhere else that has any document or files from the time period in question. I've made several [calls] to hospitals such as Corpus and nobody knows of any. They've been destroyed." On its way to issuing an evidence preclusion sanction against the United States, this exchange prompted the district court to write: "Defendant has not explained why, at this point, it did not immediately notify the court that relevant documents had been destroyed, even if under the MTFs' normal documentation retention procedures." *Id.* at **10.

[27] *Cf.* Final Report of Neal Batson, Court-Appointed Examiner, 2003 WL 22853260 (CORP-SCAN) (Bankr. S.D.N.Y. November 4, 2003). In evaluating the viability of claims of legal malpractice against Enron's in-house and outside counsel in the Enron bankruptcy, the examiner cited Texas RPC 1.12 (the equivalent to Model Rule 1.13) saying it "may be considered by a fact-finder in understanding and applying the standard of care for malpractice when that rule is designed for the protection of persons in the position of the plaintiff." The examiner argued that under Texas Rule 1.12 an attorney for an organization "must take reasonable remedial actions" that are in the best interest of the organization under circumstances covered by Texas RPC 1.12. The examiner concluded "that an attorney for Enron who knew that (i) an officer was engaging in wrongful conduct, (ii) substantial injury to Enron was likely to occur as a result of that conduct and (iii) the violation was within the attorney's scope of representation, but failed to take appropriate affirmative steps to cause reconsideration of the matter—including referral of the matter to a higher authority in the company, including, if appropriate, the Enron Board—would not have acted as an attorney of reasonable prudence would have in a similar situation." *Id.* at 14-15.

must climb the reporting ladder. What happens after this depends on the reaction of, and reaction time by, the highest authority in the organization, the specific facts, the seriousness of the matter and the pressures created thereby, and how Rule 1.13 reads or will read[28] in the state or states with jurisdiction.

---

[28] Lawyers are advised to monitor amendments to Rule 1.13 in the states since a state is not bound to accept Model Rule 1.13 in its current form.

CHAPTER FIVE

Outsourcing E-Discovery

Outsourcing work such as the review of electronically stored information to foreign-licensed lawyers or contractors may be appealing to lawyers and clients dealing with large numbers of electronic documents if the billing rates of the foreign-licensed lawyers or contractors are lower then reviewers in the United States and their work is at least as efficient and accurate as their American counterparts' work. The ethical propriety of this practice has not been directly addressed in ethics opinions, but several opinions speak to the issue of outsourcing in a variety of contexts that, by analogy, offer guidance to lawyers wondering whether outsourcing of e-discovery legal work offends the rules of professional conduct.[1]

Unauthorized Practice of Law Under Model Rule 5.5

Model Rule 5.5(a) prohibits a lawyer from practicing law in a jurisdiction in violation of the regulation of the legal profession in that jurisdiction, or to "assist another in doing so."

Model Rule 5.5(b) provides that a nonadmitted lawyer in a particular jurisdiction "shall not":

> (1) except as authorized by these Rules or other law, establish an office or other systematic and continuous presence in this jurisdiction for the practice of law; or
> (2) hold out to the public or otherwise represent that the lawyer is admitted to practice law in this jurisdiction.

[1] Links to the opinions are provided below and also in Appendix III.

Model Rule 5.5(c) allows lawyers "admitted in another United States jurisdiction," and not disbarred or suspended in another jurisdiction, to provide certain legal services "on a temporary basis" in "this jurisdiction" under certain circumstances.[2]

In dealing with outsourcing, the focus of the ethics opinions has been on "assisting" another to practice law in the retaining lawyer's jurisdiction.

When issuing its Opinion 07-02 (January 18, 2008),[3] the Florida Bar's Professional Ethics Committee elected not to answer the question of whether outsourcing legal work, including "litigation support," "to overseas attorneys or paralegals" constitutes "assisting in the unlicensed practice of law" prohibited by Florida RPC 4-5.5. In defining "the practice of law," the committee focused on the protection of the public from "incompetent, unethical, or irresponsible representation,"[4] and decided that it was not "authorized" to make the determination "whether or not the proposed activities constitute the unlicensed practice of law." Rather, it told the inquiring lawyer "to determine whether activities (legal work)

---

[2] There are four circumstances identified in Model Rule 5.5(c). The legal services "(1) are undertaken in association with a lawyer who is admitted to practice in this jurisdiction and who actively participates in the matter; (2) are in or reasonably related to a pending or potential proceeding before a tribunal in this or another jurisdiction, if the lawyer, or a person the lawyer is assisting, is authorized by law or order to appear in such proceeding or reasonably expects to be so authorized; (3) are in or reasonably related to a pending or potential arbitration, mediation, or other alternative dispute resolution proceeding in this or another jurisdiction, if the services arise out of or are reasonably related to the lawyer's practice in a jurisdiction in which the lawyer is admitted to practice and are not services for which the forum requires *pro hac vice* admission; or (4) are not within paragraphs (c)(2) or (c)(3) and arise out of or are reasonably related to the lawyer's practice in a jurisdiction in which the lawyer is admitted to practice." Model Rule 5.5(d) also allows a lawyer "admitted in another United States jurisdiction, and not disbarred or suspended from practice in any jurisdiction," to provide legal services "in this jurisdiction that: (1) are provided to the lawyer's employer or its organizational affiliates and are not services for which the forum requires *pro hac vice* admission; or (2) are services that the lawyer is authorized to provide by federal law or other law of this jurisdiction."

[3] Http://www.floridabar.org/TFB/TFBResources.nsf/Attachments/DB3E4EDA068D91738 52573530070B8D0/$FILE/07-2%20pao.pdf?OpenElement. The opinion was approved by the Florida Bar Board of Governors on July 25, 2008.

[4] The ethics committee quoted from The Florida Bar v. Moses, 380 So.2d. 412, 417 (Fla. 1980) in explaining that when evaluating whether an activity represents the practice of law, "'the single most important concern in the Court's defining and regulating the practice of law is the protection of the public from incompetent, unethical, or irresponsible representation.'"

being undertaken or assigned to others might violate Rule 4-5.5 and any applicable rule of law."

The Committee on Professional and Judicial Ethics of the Association of the Bar of the City of New York was not as shy. In its Formal Opinion 2006-3 (August 2006),[5] the committee answered the question of whether a New York lawyer may outsource legal support services to a foreign lawyer not admitted to practice in the United States or to a lay person. Applying DR 3-101(A) of the Model Code of Professional Responsibility—which prohibits a lawyer from aiding a nonlawyer in the unauthorized practice of law—the committee determined that as long as the lawyer supervises the foreign lawyer's work, there is no ethical violation. To emphasize the level of supervision required, the committee concluded:

> The potential benefits resulting from a lawyer's delegating work to a non-lawyer cannot be denied. But at the same time, to avoid aiding the unauthorized practice of law, the lawyer must at every step shoulder complete responsibility for the non-lawyer's work. In short, the lawyer must, by applying professional skill and judgment, first set the appropriate scope for the non-lawyer's work and then vet the non-lawyer's work and ensure its quality.

This determination is consistent with similar opinions issued by other bar association ethics committees, albeit under different circumstances. For example, in Opinion 518 (June 19, 2006),[6] the Los Angeles County Bar Association determined that a lawyer who contracted with an out-of-state company to draft a brief on behalf of a client was not assisting in the violation of the California Rules of Professional Conduct "so long as the attorney remains ultimately responsible for the final work product provided to or on behalf of the client."

Similarly, in Opinion 2007-01,[7] the San Diego County Bar Association confronted the question of whether a lawyer retained to handle an intellectual property matter in which the lawyer had limited experience could ethically retain Legalworks, a firm in India, to do legal research, develop a case strategy, and prepare motions, among other tasks. Ultimately, the lawyer's summary judgment motion was granted, after which the lawyer disclosed to the client that the lawyer had used the Indian firm to do

[5] Http://www.nycbar.org/Ethics/eth2006.htm.

[6] Http://www.lacba.org/Files/Main%20Folder/Documents/%20Ethics%20%20%20Opinions/Files/Ethics_Opinion_518.pdf.

[7] Http://www.sdcba.org/ethics/ethicsopinion07-1.htm.

the bulk of the work. Did the lawyer aid the unauthorized practice of law? The SDCBA determined that the lawyer had not:

> The California lawyer in this case retained full control over the representation of the client and exercised independent judgment in reviewing the draft work performed by those who were not California attorneys. His fiduciary duties and potential liability to his corporate client for all of the legal work that was performed were undiluted by the assistance he obtained from Legalworks. In short, in the usual arrangement, and in the scenario described above in particular, the company to whom work was outsourced has assisted the California lawyer in practicing law in this state, not the other way around. And that is not prohibited.

The ABA's Standing Committee on Professional Ethics and Professional Responsibility addressed outsourcing in Formal Opinion 08-451 (August 5, 2008) and ended its discussion with a reference to Model Rule 5.5(a)'s prohibition on assisting others in the unauthorized practice of law. While not taking a stand, the committee suggested that proper supervision would eliminate the risk: "This Committee lacks the authority to express an opinion as to whether the provision of legal services by any particular lawyer, nonlawyer, or intermediary constitutes the unauthorized practice of law. Ordinarily, an individual who is not admitted to practice law in a particular jurisdiction may work for a lawyer who is so admitted, provided that the lawyer remains responsible for the work being performed and that the individual is not held out as being a duly admitted lawyer." The committee reminded outsourcing lawyers, however, that "if the activities of a lawyer, nonlawyer, or intermediary employed in an outsourcing capacity are held to be the unauthorized practice of law, and the outsourcing lawyer facilitated that violation of law by action or inaction, the outsourcing lawyer will have violated Rule 5.5(a)."

With appropriate supervision and control, outsourcing should not violate Model Rule 5.5 or its analog in those states that have adopted it.

Competence Under Model Rule 1.1

ABA Formal Opinion 08-451 covers a number of rules of professional conduct beyond Model Rule 5.5, and its analysis is sure to find its way into both state bar ethics opinions and future court decisions on the propriety of outsourcing. ABA Opinion 08-451's initial focus was on Model Rule 1.1, explaining that there is nothing unethical about outsourcing legal and nonlegal services provided that the outsourcing lawyer satisfies

Model Rule 1.1's requirement that a lawyer have the "legal knowledge, skill, thoroughness, and preparation reasonably necessary" to represent a client. Competence does not mean, the ABA Standing Committee wrote, that lawyers must do the work themselves. Rather, Model Rule 1.1 "requires only that the lawyer who is responsible to the client satisfies her obligations to render legal services competently."

Duty to Supervise Under Model Rules 5.1 and 5.3

As discussed earlier, Model Rules 5.1 and 5.3(a) and (b) require a lawyer having direct supervisory authority over a subordinate lawyers or nonlawyers, respectively, to make reasonable efforts to ensure that that their conduct is compatible with the professional obligations of the lawyer. Under Model Rule 5.1(c), a lawyer is responsible for a subordinate lawyer's violation of the Rules of Professional Conduct, and under Model Rule 5.3(c), a lawyer is responsible for the conduct of the nonlawyer that, in both cases, "would be a violation of the Rules of Professional Conduct if engaged in by a lawyer," if (1) the lawyer orders the conduct, or with the knowledge of the specific conduct, ratifies the conduct, or (2) the lawyer "knows of the conduct at a time when its consequences can be avoided or mitigated but fails to take reasonable remedial action."[8]

ABA Formal Opinion 08-451 quickly moved to Model Rules 5.1 and 5.3 in evaluating an outsourcing lawyer's ethical obligations. The Standing Committee offered a menu of ideas for a lawyer's consideration when outsourcing services for "ultimate provision to a client":

1. Conduct reference checks and investigate the background of the lawyer or nonlawyer providing the services, as well as any nonlawyer intermediary involved such as a placement agency or service provider.
2. Interview the principal lawyers, if any, involved in the project, and, among other things, assess their educational background.

[8] It seems unnecessary to note that the duty to supervise presupposes the competence to supervise, as is required by Model Rule 1.1. *See, e.g.*, San Diego Bar Association Ethics Op. 2007-1 (hiring firm in India to assist in defending intellectual property case required sufficient experience in the retaining attorney to perform a critical and independent evaluation of the work product produced by the Indian firm).

3. When dealing with an intermediary, inquire into its hiring practices "to evaluate the quality and character of the employees likely to have access to client information."
4. Depending on the sensitivity of the information being provided to the service provider, "investigate the security of the provider's premises, computer network, and perhaps even its recycling and refuse disposal procedures."
5. When prudent, "pay a personal visit to the intermediary's facility, regardless of its location or the difficulty of travel, to get a firsthand sense of its operation and the professionalism of the lawyers and nonlawyers it is procuring."
6. When engaging lawyers trained in a foreign country, assess "whether the system of legal education under which the lawyers were trained is comparable to that in the United States."[9]
7. Evaluate the professional regulatory system "to determine whether members of the nation's legal profession have been inculcated with core ethical principles similar to those in the United States, and whether the nation's disciplinary enforcement system is effective in policing its lawyers."[10]
8. Pay attention to "the legal landscape of the nation to which the services are being outsourced, particularly the extent that personal property, including documents, may be susceptible to seizure in judicial or administrative proceedings notwithstanding claims of client confidentiality."
9. Evaluate the judicial system of the country in question "to assess the risk of loss of client information or disruption of the project in the event that a dispute arises between the service provider and the lawyer and the courts do not provide prompt and effective remedies to avert prejudice to the client."

In its Opinion 07-2 (January 18, 2008), the Florida Bar Ethics Committee explained that Florida's RPC 4-5.3 applies to the conduct of "overseas providers." In an apparent effort to identify the lawyer's obligations, the

[9] The ABA Standing Committee explained that, "In some nations, people can call themselves 'lawyers' with only a minimal level of training."

[10] The ABA Standing Committee was quick to add that its motive was self-protective for lawyers: "The lack of rigorous training or effective lawyer discipline does not mean that individuals from that nation cannot be engaged to work on a particular project. What it does mean is that, in such circumstances, it will be more important than ever for the outsourcing lawyer to scrutinize the work done by the foreign lawyers—perhaps viewing them as nonlawyers—before relying upon their work in rendering legal services to the client."

committee quoted from the comment to the Florida version of Model Rule 5.3:

> A lawyer must give such assistants appropriate instruction and supervision concerning the ethical aspects of their employment, particularly regarding the obligation not to disclose information relating to representation of the client. The measures employed in supervising nonlawyers should take account of the level of their legal training and the fact that they are not subject to professional discipline. If an activity requires the independent judgment and participation of the lawyer, it cannot be properly delegated to a nonlawyer employee.

In dealing with the use of the Legalworks firm in India, the San Diego Bar Association, in its Ethics Opinion 2007-1, cited to ABA Model Rule 5.1 in explaining that the lawyer "also retains ultimate responsibility for that work."[11]

In analyzing the ethical propriety of outsourcing legal work overseas, the City of New York Bar Ethics Committee offered a number of suggestions to lawyers obliged to satisfy their ethical duty to supervise.

> Although each situation is different, among the salutary steps in discharging the duty to supervise that the New York lawyer should consider are to (a) obtain background information about any intermediary employing or engaging the non-lawyer, and obtain the professional résumé of the non-lawyer; (b) conduct reference checks; (c) interview the non-lawyer in advance, for example, by telephone or by voice-over-internet protocol or by web cast, to ascertain the particular non-lawyer's suitability for the particular assignment; and (d) communicate with the non-lawyer during the assignment to ensure that the non-lawyer understands the assignment and that the non-lawyer is discharging the assignment according to the lawyer's expectations.[12]

---

[11] Http://www.sdcba.org/ethics/ethicsopinion07-1.htm: "By retaining responsibility for the work, the supervising attorney is subject to the ABA Model Rules that hold a lawyer responsible for another lawyer's violation of professional responsibility rules where: 1) the lawyer orders or ratifies the misconduct; or where 2) the lawyer has supervisory authority over the other lawyer and knows of the conduct at the time when the consequences could have been avoided or mitigated but failed to take remedial action. (ABA Model Rule 5.1(c) & Comment 5.)"

[12] Http://www.nycbar.org/Ethics/eth2006.htm.

In short, the retaining lawyer must know with whom the lawyer is dealing, and will retain responsibility for the outsourced provider's work.

Avoiding Conflicts of Interest Under Model Rule 1.7

Model Rule 1.7 prohibits representation of a client if the representation involves a concurrent conflict of interest:

> (a) Except as provided in paragraph (b), a lawyer shall not represent a client if the representation involves a concurrent conflict of interest. A concurrent conflict of interest exists if:
>
> (1) the representation of one client will be directly adverse to another client; or
>
> (2) there is a significant risk that the representation of one or more clients will be materially limited by the lawyer's responsibilities to another client, a former client or a third person or by a personal interest of the lawyer.

Protecting against conflicts is another obligation of lawyers that the ethics opinions issued to date on the subject of outsourcing have identified. The Florida Bar Ethics Committee relied on Opinion 518 from the Los Angeles County Bar Association, which described the lawyer's obligation regarding conflicts of interest in retaining a nonlicensed lawyer to perform work for a client:

> [T]he attorney should satisfy himself that no conflicts exist that would preclude the representation. [Cite omitted.] The attorney must also recognize that he or she could be held responsible for any conflict of interest that may be created by the hiring of Company and which could arise from relationships that Company develops with others during the attorney's relationship with Company.[13]

The City of New York Bar Ethics Opinion 2006-3 provides similar guidance:

> As a threshold matter, the outsourcing New York lawyer should ask the intermediary, which employs or engages the overseas non-lawyer, about its conflict-checking procedures and about how it tracks work performed for other clients. The outsourcing New York

[13] Florida Bar Ethics Op. 07-2 (January 18, 2008, as modified on July 25, 2008), http://www.floridabar.org/TFB/TFBResources.nsf/Attachments/DB3E4EDA068D9173852573530070B8D0/$FILE/07-2%20pao.pdf?OpenElement, *quoting from* Los Angeles County Bar Ethics Op. 518 (June 19, 2006), http://www.lacba.org/Files/Main%20Folder/Documents/%20Ethics%20%20%20Opinions/Files/Ethics_Opinion_518.pdf.

> lawyer should also ordinarily ask both the intermediary and the non-lawyer performing the legal support service whether either is performing, or has performed, services for any parties adverse to the lawyer's client. The outsourcing New York lawyer should pursue further inquiry as required, while also reminding both the intermediary and the non-lawyer, preferably in writing, of the need for them to safeguard the confidences and secrets of their other current and former clients.

As required by the rules of professional conduct, and as explained in the City of New York Bar's Ethics Opinion 2006-3, avoiding conflicts goes hand in hand with protecting confidences of the client, a subject to which I next turn.

The Duty of Confidentiality Under Model Rule 1.6

We have already discussed Model Rule 1.6. As a reminder, Rule 1.6(a) provides that a lawyer "shall not" reveal information "relating to representation of a client unless the client gives informed consent," the disclosure is "impliedly authorized in order to carry out the representation," or the disclosure is permitted by Rule 1.6(b).

The lawyer using outside contractors must ensure that the outside contractors "agree to keep client confidences and secrets inviolate." Los Angeles County Bar Ethics Opinion 518, p. 14.[14] In the context of outsourcing legal work, the City of New York Bar Ethics Opinion 2006-03 again offers guidance on steps to take to preserve client confidences:

> Measures that New York lawyers may take to help preserve client confidences and secrets when outsourcing overseas include restricting access to confidences and secrets, contractual provisions addressing confidentiality and remedies in the event of breach, and periodic reminders regarding confidentiality.[15]

Florida Bar Ethics Opinion 07-2 elaborates on possible safeguards the lawyer should employ in the context of transmission of information electronically to an overseas contractor.

---

[14] *Cf.* Formal Op. 2004-165 of the California State Bar Standing Committee on Professional Responsibility and Conduct (a lawyer that uses on a contract basis a court appearance service operated by lawyers must take precautions "to assure" that information "imparted to the appearing lawyer is held in confidence." Https://www.lexisnexis.com/applieddiscovery/LawLibrary/CourtRulesArticles/CAstatebarop.pdf.

[15] Http://www.nycbar.org/Ethics/eth2006.htm. In its Ethics Op. 07-2, the Florida Bar Ethics Committee endorsed this part of the City of New York Bar Ethics Op. 2006-03.

> [A]ssurances by the foreign provider that policies and processes are employed to protect the data while in transit, at rest, in use, and post-provision of services should be set forth in sufficient detail for the requesting attorney. Moreover, foreign data-breach and identity protection laws and remedies, where such exist at all, may differ substantially in both scope and coverage from U.S. Federal and State laws and regulations. In light of such differing rules and regulations, an attorney should require sufficient and specific assurances (together with an outline of relevant policies and processes) that the data, once used for the service requested, will be irretrievably destroyed, and not sold, used, or otherwise be capable of access after the provision of the contracted-for service. While the foregoing issues are likewise applicable to domestic service providers, they present a heightened supervisory and auditability concern in foreign (i.e., non-U.S.) jurisdictions, and should be accorded heightened scrutiny by the attorney seeking to use such services.[16]

ABA Formal Opinion 08-451 also weighs in on protecting confidentiality of client information. It suggests execution of a confidentiality agreement and a conflict check:

> Also, the outsourcing lawyer should be mindful of the obligation to 'act competently to safeguard information relating to the representation of a client against inadvertent or unauthorized disclosure by the lawyer or other persons who are participating in the representation of the client or who are subject to the lawyer's supervision.' This requires the lawyer to recognize and minimize the risk that any outside service provider may inadvertently—or perhaps even advertently—reveal client confidential information to adverse parties or to others who are not entitled to access. Written confidentiality agreements are, therefore, strongly advisable in outsourcing relationships. Likewise, to minimize the risk of potentially wrongful disclosure, the outsourcing lawyer should verify that the

[16] In approving Ethics Op. 07-2, the Board of Governors of the Florida Bar approved the addition of one additional paragraph to account for handling sensitive information of third parties or opposing parties: "In addition to concerns regarding the confidentiality of client information, there are concerns about disclosure of sensitive information of others, such as an opposing party or third party. In outsourcing, there is the possibility that information of others will be disclosed in addition to the disclosure of client information. Lawyers should be mindful of any obligations under law regarding disclosure of sensitive information of opposing parties and third parties, particularly where the information concerns medical records or financial information."

outside service provider does not also do work for adversaries of their clients on the same or substantially related matters; in such an instance, the outsourcing lawyer could choose another provider.

ABA Formal Opinion 08-451 (quoting from Model Rule 1.6, cmt. 16; footnote omitted).

Outsourcing overseas must be accompanied by confidentiality safeguards to protect the client, which, in turn raises the question of the client's role in deciding to outsource e-discovery work to an overseas provider.

Must a Client's Informed Consent Be Obtained Before Outsourcing E-Discovery Work?

Model Rule 1.6(a) prohibits a lawyer from revealing information relating to the representation of a client unless the client gives "informed consent." As noted earlier, Model Rule 1.0(e) defines informed consent as denoting "the agreement by a person to a proposed course of conduct after the lawyer has communicated adequate information and explanation about the material risks of and reasonably available alternatives to the proposed course of conduct."

ABA Formal Opinion 08-451 addresses protection of confidential client information. Explaining that an outsourcing relationship is typically an attenuated one in contrast with other relationships between lawyers and individuals who perform services for a lawyer, it bluntly admonishes: "no information protected by Rule 1.6 may be revealed without the client's informed consent. The implied authorization of Rule 1.6(a) and its Comment [5] thereto to share confidential information within a firm does not extend to outside entities or to individuals over whom the firm lacks effective supervision and control."

Short of sharing confidential information, ABA Formal Opinion 08-451 takes a measured approach controlled in part by precedent. The Standing Committee first explained that in its Formal Opinion 88-356 (Dec. 16, 1988). The committee opined "that when a lawyer engaged the services of a temporary lawyer, a form of outsourcing, an obligation to advise the client of that fact and to seek the client's consent would arise if the temporary lawyer was to perform independent work for the client without the close supervision of the hiring lawyer or another lawyer associated with her firm."[17] Second, the committee noted that a lawyer

[17] The committee also explained its thinking: "Relying on Rule 1.2(a), requiring lawyers to consult with clients as to the means by which the clients' objectives are to be pursued, Rule

may not, under Model Rules 7.1 and 8.4(c)[18] make affirmative misrepresentations to the client regarding the status of lawyers and nonlawyers who are not in the lawyer's employ. The committee acknowledged that Formal Opinion 88-356 ultimately held that the client ordinarily is not entitled to notice that its legal work is being performed by a temporary lawyer, but it said this conclusion was premised "on the assumption that the relationship between the firm and the temporary lawyer involved a high degree of supervision and control, so that the temporary lawyer would be tantamount to an employee, subject to discipline or even firing for misconduct." In contrast, an outsourcing relationship would not, the Standing Committee stated, ordinarily involve this level of supervision and control, "particularly in a relationship involving outsourcing through an intermediary that itself has the employment relationship with the lawyers or nonlawyers in question." In the end, the Standing Committee concluded only that it "may be necessary" to provide information to the client concerning the outsourcing relationship and "perhaps" to obtain the client's informed consent.

Other ethics opinions addressing outsourcing relate the obligation to obtain informed consent to the role of the outsourcing contractor and the risk involved. Florida Bar Ethics Opinion 07-2 explains:

> The requirement for informed consent from a client should be generally commensurate with the degree of risk involved in the contemplated activity for which such consent is sought.
>
> ***
>
> The committee believes that the law firm should obtain prior client consent to disclose information that the firm reasonably believes is necessary to serve the client's interests. Rule 4-1.6 (c)(1), Rules Regulating The Florida Bar.[19] In determining whether a client should be

---

1.4, relating to client communication, and Rule 7.5(d), prohibiting lawyers from implying that they practice in a partnership or other organization when that is not the fact, we concluded that clients are entitled to know who or what entity is representing them, and thus could veto the lawyer's use of a temporary lawyer."

[18] Model Rule 7.1 requires truthfulness in communications regarding lawyer services. Model Rule 8.4(c) was defined earlier and states that it is professional misconduct for a lawyer to engage in conduct involving dishonesty, fraud, deceit, or misrepresentation.

[19] Florida's Rule of Professional Conduct 4-1.6 (a) provides in pertinent part that that a lawyer "shall not reveal information relating to representation of a client except as stated in [subdivision] . . . (c), . . . , unless the client gives informed consent." Florida's Rule of Professional Conduct 4-1.6(c)(1) then provides that, "A lawyer may reveal such information to the extent the lawyer reasonably believes necessary: (1) to serve the client's interest unless it is information the client specifically requires not to be disclosed." The Florida

> informed of the participation of the overseas provider an attorney should bear in mind factors such as whether a client would reasonably expect the lawyer or law firm to personally handle the matter and whether the non-lawyers will have more than a limited role in the provision of the services. For example, in Opinion 88-12, we stated that a law firm's use of a temporary lawyer may need to be disclosed to a client if the client would likely consider the information to be material.

The City of New York Bar Ethics Opinion 2006-3 also contrasted the use of temporary lawyers with the referral of work to an overseas nonlawyer contractor in offering this guidance:

> Non-lawyers often play more limited roles in matters than contract or temporary lawyers do. Thus, there is little purpose in requiring a lawyer to reflexively inform a client every time that the lawyer intends to outsource legal support services overseas to a non-lawyer. But the presence of one or more additional considerations may alter the analysis: for example, if (a) non-lawyers will play a significant role in the matter, e.g., several non-lawyers are being hired to do an important document review; (b) client confidences and secrets must be shared with the non-lawyer, in which case informed advance consent should be secured from the client; (c) the client expects that only personnel employed by the law firm will handle the matter; or (d) non-lawyers are to be billed to the client on a basis other than cost, in which case the client's informed advance consent is needed.

The opinion writers were explicit about when a client confidence or secret has to be disclosed: "We conclude that if the outsourcing assignment requires the lawyer to disclose client confidences or secrets to the overseas nonlawyer, then the lawyer should secure the client's informed consent in advance. In this regard, the lawyer must be mindful that different laws and traditions regarding the confidentiality of client information obtain overseas."[20]

Rules of Professional Conduct can be found at http://www.floridabar.org/divexe/rrtfb.nsf/WContents?OpenView&Start=1&Count=30&Expand=4.

[20] The opinion writers here cited N.Y. State Op. 762 (2003), characterizing it as determining that "a New York law firm must explain to a client represented by lawyers in foreign offices of the firm the extent to which confidentiality rules in those foreign jurisdictions provide less protection than in New York." This opinion can be found at http://www.nysba.org/AM/Template.cfm?Section=Ethics_Opinions&TEMPLATE=/CM/ContentDisplay.cfm&CONTENTID=13596.

In Ethics Opinion 2007-1, in the context of the use of Legalworks, a firm in India that assisted the lawyer in defending an intellectual property lawsuit, the San Diego County Bar Association framed the issue of client consent in terms of the expectation of the client with respect to the services provided by a lawyer:

> [T]he duty to inform the client is determined by the client's reasonable expectation as to who will perform those services. Therefore, if the work which is to be performed by the outside service is within the client's "reasonable expectation under the circumstances" that it will be performed by the attorney, the client must be informed when the service is "outsourced." Conversely, if the service is not a service that is within the client's reasonable expectation that it will be performed by the attorney, the attorney is not necessarily required to inform the client immediately, absent other requirements compelling disclosure.

Cf. Los Angeles County Bar Association Ethics Opinion 518, p. 6 (in the context of the use of an out-of-state company to write a brief for the lawyer, explaining that a lawyer has a duty to keep a client informed of significant developments relating to the representation and whether the use of an outside lawyer constitutes a significant development "is based upon the circumstances of each case").[21]

The facts dictate the obligation. For example, it is unlikely that a lawyer would outsource overseas the review of electronically stored information pursuant to work-product-protected protocols without involvement of the client. To even consider the option presupposes that there is a cost savings by outsourcing the work and there are sufficient numbers of files that costs, in fact, can be saved by outsourcing.[22] Typically, these are joint lawyer-client decisions.

[21] The Los Angeles County Bar Association cited Formal Op. 2004-165 of California's Office of Professional Responsibility and Conduct, which explained that California's Rule 3-500 provides that a member of the California Bar must keep a client "reasonably informed about significant developments relating to the employment or representation." *See* https://www.lexisnexis.com/applieddiscovery/LawLibrary/CourtRulesArticles/CAstatebarop.pdf, at 2.

[22] No e-discovery restoration, retrieval, and review process is going to be error free. The goal is to get it as right as one reasonably can the first time in all three respects. Within this context of reasonableness, whether there is a cost savings is not just a function of billing rate but also of training time, efficiency, and accuracy.

Billing for Outsourced Services

Model Rule 1.5(a) provides that, "A lawyer shall not make an agreement for, charge, or collect an unreasonable fee or an unreasonable amount for expenses." Model Rule 1.5(a) adds that the factors to be considered in determining the reasonableness of a fee include the following:

> (1) the time and labor required, the novelty and difficulty of the questions involved, and the skill requisite to perform the legal service properly; (2) the likelihood, if apparent to the client, that the acceptance of the particular employment will preclude other employment by the lawyer; (3) the fee customarily charged in the locality for similar legal services; (4) the amount involved and the results obtained; (5) the time limitations imposed by the client or by the circumstances; (6) the nature and length of the professional relationship with the client; (7) the experience, reputation, and ability of the lawyer or lawyers performing the services; and (8) whether the fee is fixed or contingent.[23]

Model Rule 1.5(b) adds that the scope of the representation and the basis or rate of the fee and expenses for which the client will be responsible "shall be communicated to the client, preferably in writing, before or within a reasonable time after commencing the representation, except when the lawyer will charge a regularly represented client on the same basis or rate. Any changes in the basis or rate of the fee or expenses shall also be communicated to the client."

Relying on the prohibition against fee-splitting with a nonlawyer in the Model Code of Professional Responsibility, in Formal Opinion 2006-03, the City of New York Bar addressed charges for outsourcing legal support services[24] to an overseas nonlawyer:

---

[23] Comment [1] to Model Rule 1.5(a) explains that the factors "specified in (1) through (8) are not exclusive. Nor will each factor be relevant in each instance." With respect to expenses, it adds that, "A lawyer may seek reimbursement for the cost of services performed in-house, such as copying, or for other expenses incurred in-house, such as telephone charges, either by charging a reasonable amount to which the client has agreed in advance or by charging an amount that reasonably reflects the cost incurred by the lawyer."

[24] According to note 4 of the City of New York Bar's Formal Op. 2006-3, the opinion concerns outsourcing of "'substantive legal support services,' which includes legal research, drafting, due diligence reports, patent and trademark work, review of transactional and litigation documents, and drafting contracts, pleadings, or memoranda of law. This is distinguished from 'administrative legal support services,' which include transcription of voice files from depositions, trials and hearings; accounting support in the preparation of timesheets and billing materials; paralegal and clerical support for file manage-

> By definition, the non-lawyer performing legal support services overseas is not performing legal services. It is thus inappropriate for the New York lawyer to include the cost of outsourcing in his or her legal fees. *See* DR 3-102.[25] Absent a specific agreement with the client to the contrary, the lawyer should charge the client no more than the direct cost associated with outsourcing, plus a reasonable allocation of overhead expenses directly associated with providing that service. ABA Formal Opinion 93-379 (1993).

Without citing to a rule of professional conduct, the Florida Bar's Ethics Opinion 07-2 also addressed billing under the facts presented, stating:

> The law firm may charge a client the actual cost of the overseas provider, unless the charge would normally be covered as overhead. However, in a contingent fee case, it would be improper to charge separately for work that is usually otherwise accomplished by a client's own attorney and incorporated into the standard fee paid to the attorney, even if that cost is paid to a third party provider.

Opinion 518 of the Los Angeles County Bar Association, which addressed the retention by a lawyer of an out-of-state company to draft a brief, explains that the lawyer could pay the cost of the brief without passing on any of the cost to the client, or may elect to pass the cost on to the client directly for payment, mark up the cost and pass it on to the client, or charge the client a flat fee.[26]

ABA Formal Opinion 08-451 states that the "fees charged by the outsourcing lawyer must be reasonable and otherwise comply with the requirements of Rule 1.5." Citing precedent,[27] the ABA Standing Committee appeared to bless the addition of a surcharge to the outsourcing costs paid by the billing lawyer as long as the total charge to the client

ment; litigation support graphics; and data entry for marketing, conflicts, and contact management."

[25] DR 3-102 provides that a lawyer shall not share legal fees with a nonlawyer.

[26] Http://www.lacba.org/Files/Main%20Folder/Documents/%20Ethics%20%20%20Opinions/Files/Ethics_Opinion_518.pdf, at 10-11. The Ethics Committee of the Los Angeles County Bar added that the attorney "must accurately disclose the basis upon which any cost is passed on to the client." *Id.* at 12. In Ethics Opinion 2007-1, the San Diego County Bar Association explained that the lawyer who retained Legalworks, a firm in India, to help the lawyer defend an intellectual property case had billed the client for the actual cost of the use of the firm.

[27] ABA Comm. on Ethics and Prof'l Responsibility, Formal Op. 00-420 (Nov. 29, 2000) ("a law firm that engaged a contract lawyer could add a surcharge to the cost paid by the billing lawyer provided the total charge represented a reasonable fee for the services provided to the client").

represented a "reasonable fee" for the services provided to the client. The Standing Committee reasoned as follows:

> This is not substantively different from the manner in which a conventional law firm bills for the services of its lawyers. The firm pays a lawyer a salary, provides him with employment benefits, incurs office space and other overhead costs to support him, and also earns a profit from his services; the client generally is not informed of the details of the financial relationship between the law firm and the lawyer. Likewise, the lawyer is not obligated to inform the client how much the firm is paying a contract lawyer; the restraint is the overarching requirement that the fee charged for the services not be unreasonable.

On the other hand, if the outsourcing fees are treated as a law firm disbursement, "no markup is permitted." The Standing Committee explained:

> In the absence of an agreement with the client authorizing a greater charge, the lawyer may bill the client only its actual cost plus a reasonable allocation of associated overhead, such as the amount the lawyer spent on any office space, support staff, equipment, and supplies for the individuals under contract. The analysis is no different for other outsourced legal services, except that the overhead costs associated with the provision of such services may be minimal or nonexistent if and to the extent that the outsourced work is performed off-site without the need for infrastructural support. If that is true, the outsourced services should be billed at cost, plus a reasonable allocation of the cost of supervising those services if not otherwise covered by the fees being charged for legal services.

ABA Formal Opinion 08-451 (footnote omitted).

Depending on whether outsourcing involves nonlawyers or fee splitting, the jurisdiction, and the specific facts relating to the services outsourced, a reasonableness standard governs the billing arrangement for legal services outsourced overseas, subject to any agreement between the lawyer and the client on billing for these services.

CHAPTER SIX

Conclusion

This journey through ethical issues in e-discovery has no places to rest. When you are on the e-discovery ethics track, if you lay down your guard, you will get run over. Competence is the place to start, but candor is always the place to be. In between, I am also confident in saying that lawyers will face ethics issues beyond those covered here. This is particularly true in the era of multijurisdictional practice where—as demonstrated by the multiple and differing ethics opinions on the propriety of the review of metadata—different interpretive rules based on different rules of professional conduct may be applicable in different jurisdictions, creating uncertainty as to the rules to follow in jurisdictions which have not yet rendered interpretive rules.[1]

[1] Model Rule 5.5 permits multiple jurisdictional practice. *See, e.g.*, Ethics Docket 03-07, Maryland State Bar Association, Inc. Committee On Ethics, October 2003 (since Delaware adopted the ABA's Rule 5.5, Delaware now allows out-of-state attorneys to provide legal services in Delaware on a temporary basis, so it would not be the unauthorized practice of law for a Maryland lawyer to conduct a real estate settlement involving Delaware property in Maryland for a Maryland client). The trade-off for this privilege appears in Rule 8.5, which provides that a lawyer "not admitted in this jurisdiction" is subject to the disciplinary authority of "this jurisdiction" if the lawyer provides or offers to provide "legal services" "in this jurisdiction." Rule 22 of the ABA Model Rules for Lawyer Disciplinary Enforcement requires a jurisdiction in which a lawyer is licensed to reciprocally enforce another jurisdiction's disciplinary decision, even if the lawyer is not admitted in that other jurisdiction, unless there are public policy reasons not to approve reciprocal discipline. As these changes are adopted by states, a lawyer that is found to be engaged in the practice of law in another state will have to consider that other state's rules of professional conduct that relate to disclosure. As of November 2008, twelve jurisdictions had adopted Model Rule 5.5 verbatim and twenty-five jurisdictions had adopted a similar rule, and nineteen jurisdictions had adopted Rule 8.5 verbatim with nineteen jurisdictions adopting a similar

Prudent lawyers—whether in-house or outside counsel—will recognize when they need e-discovery advice and then obtain and follow it. In the arena of e-discovery, where the scope of "key players" can be fluid; searches can be faulted; restoration, retrieval, and review of various types of data can be in issue; forms of production may vary; metadata may be involved; backup tapes may be implicated; potentially privileged information is costly to restore, locate, and review; electronically stored information can easily be missed or lost; and vendors have to be supervised, we all need to be prudent lawyers.

rule. *See Quick Guide Chart on State Adoption of Rule 5.5* and the same link for Rule 8.5 at http://www.abanet.org/cpr/mjp/home.html.

APPENDIX I

Example of Metadata Mined From the British Government's Posting of a Dossier on Iraqi Security and Intelligence in Microsoft Word Format (June 30, 2003)

The following information is quoted from http://www.computerbytesman.com/privacy/blair.htm:

> "Richard M. Smith (rms@computerbytesman.com)
> June 30, 2003
>
> Microsoft Word documents are notorious for containing private information in file headers which people would sometimes rather not share. The British government of Tony Blair just learned this lesson the hard way.
>
> Back in February 2003, 10 Downing Street published a dossier on Iraq's security and intelligence organizations. This dossier was cited by Colin Powell in his address to the United Nations the same month. Dr. Glen Rangwala, a lecturer in politics at Cambridge University, quickly discovered that much of the material in the dossier was actually plagiarized from a U.S. researcher on Iraq.
>
> You can read Dr. Rangwala's original analysis of the dossier from Feb. 5, 2003 at this URL: http://www.casi.org.uk/discuss/2003/msg00457.html.
>
> Blair's government made one additional mistake: they published the dossier as a Microsoft Word file on their Web site. When I first heard from Dr. Rangwala about the dossier, I decided to try to learn who had worked on the document. I downloaded the Word file containing the dossier from the 10 Downing Street Web site (http://www.number-10.gov.uk/) and found the following revision log in the file:[1]

[1] There may still be older versions of Word or documents created with older versions of Word that may have this potential security issue. However, the revision log only existed in Word versions prior to Word 2003. It was removed in Word 2003 and later versions, and if a document created in older versions (e.g., Word 2000) is opened in Word 2003, the revision log is "corrupted." This was a security patch by Microsoft for Word 2003. There are other

Rev. #1: "cic22" edited file "C:\DOCUME~1\phamill\LOCALS~1\Temp\AutoRecovery save of Iraq - security.asd"

Rev. #2: "cic22" edited file "C:\DOCUME~1\phamill\LOCALS~1\Temp\AutoRecovery save of Iraq - security.asd"

Rev. #3: "cic22" edited file "C:\DOCUME~1\phamill\LOCALS~1\Temp\AutoRecovery save of Iraq - security.asd"

Rev. #4: "JPratt" edited file "C:\TEMP\Iraq - security.doc"

Rev. #5: "JPratt" edited file "A:\Iraq - security.doc"

Rev. #6: "ablackshaw" edited file "C:\ABlackshaw\Iraq - security.doc"

Rev. #7: "ablackshaw" edited file "C:\ABlackshaw\A;Iraq - security.doc"

Rev. #8: "ablackshaw" edited file "A:\Iraq - security.doc"

Rev. #9: "MKhan" edited file "C:\TEMP\Iraq - security.doc"

Rev. #10: "MKhan" edited file "C:\WINNT\Profiles\mkhan\Desktop\Iraq.doc"

Most Word document files contain a revision log which is a listing of the last 10 edits of a document, showing the names of the people who worked with the document and the names of the files that the document went under. Revision logs are hidden and cannot be viewed in Microsoft Word. However I wrote a small utility for extracting and displaying revision logs and other hidden information in Word .DOC files.

It is easy to spot the following four names in the revision log of the Blair dossier:

P. Hamill
J. Pratt
A. Blackshaw
M. Khan

In addition, the "cic22" in the first three entries of the revision log stands for "Communications Information Centre," a unit of the British Government.

---

revisions that can be captured if the user sets Word to "save prior versions" or if the "track changes" feature was activated. Sometimes using "allow fast saves" may also leave hidden text from a prior version in a Word document that can be discovered later. "Save prior versions" doesn't exist in Word 2007 and Microsoft disabled the fast save option with Service Pack 3 of Office 2003. Personal Communication with Arlen Tanner, Esq. (April 22, 2008).

Back in February, I passed along these 4 names to Dr. Rangwala who then provided them to a number of reports in the UK. One reporter quickly identified the four individuals as:

Paul Hamill - Foreign Office official
John Pratt - Downing Street official
Alison Blackshaw - The personal assistant of the Prime Minister's press secretary
Murtaza Khan - Junior press officer for the Prime Minister

During the week of June 23, 2003, the British Parliament held hearings of the Blair Dossier and other PR efforts by the UK Government leading up to the Iraq war. Alastair Campbell of the UK Communications Information Centre was put in the hot seat and had to explain the dossier plagiarism and details of the revision log.

One of the interesting tidbits that came out of the hearings is that John Pratt provided the dossier on a floppy disk to Alison Blackshaw to give to Colin Powell for his presentation before the United Nations. The revision log shows the document being copied from Pratt's hard drive to a floppy disk in revisions #4 and #5.

The Word version of the dossier was recently removed from the 10 Downing Street Web site, but I archived a copy of the Feb. 6 version here:

IRAQ - ITS INFRASTRUCTURE OF CONCEALMENT, DECEPTION AND INTIMIDATION

http://www.computerbytesman.com/privacy/blair.doc

The Blair government learned its lesson well with regard to publishing Microsoft Word documents. Another report on Iraq that was published in June 2003 was only available as a PDF file.

As a general rule, Word document files which are converted to RTF files, HTML files, or PDF files will not contain revision logs and other metadata."

APPENDIX II

Table of Excerpts from Ethics Opinions on the Duty of Senders of Electronic Documents

Jurisdiction	Opinion
Alabama Ethics Op. 2007-02	"As such, the Commission believes that an attorney has an ethical duty to exercise reasonable care when transmitting electronic documents to ensure that he or she does not disclose his or her client's secrets and confidences. The determination of whether an attorney exercised reasonable care will, of course, vary according to the circumstances of each individual case. Factors in determining whether reasonable care was exercised may include steps taken by the attorney to prevent the disclosure of metadata, the nature and scope of the metadata revealed, the subject matter of the document, and the intended recipient. For example, an attorney would need to exercise greater care in submitting an electronic document to an opposing party than he or she would if e-filing a pleading with the court. There is simply a much higher likelihood that an adverse party would attempt to mine metadata, than a neutral and detached court."
Arizona Ethics Op. 07-03	"'When transmitting a communication that includes information relating to the representation of a client, the lawyer must take reasonable precautions to prevent the information from coming into the hands of unintended recipients.' ER 1.6, cmt 20. What is 'reasonable' in the circumstances depends on the sensitivity of the information, the potential consequences of its inadvertent disclosure, whether further disclosure

is restricted by statute, protective order, or confidentiality agreement, and any special instructions given by the client. *Id. See also* Ala. Op. RO-2007-02 (March 14, 2007); Fla. Op. 06-2 (September 15, 2006); N.Y. State Bar Op. 782 (December 8, 2004). In the case of a lawyer who is employed by a corporation or by a governmental or other entity, 'special instructions given by the client' might include the client's informed consent to forego, for financial or other reasons, the acquisition or use of software that is designed to remove metadata from an electronic document. If a lawyer is asked to comment on a document prepared by another lawyer in the firm, and the commenting lawyer knows or reasonably should know that the document is ultimately intended for transmission to opposing counsel, he or she should consider whether the comment is the type that should be included within the draft. A lawyer who prepares a pleading, contract, or other document should use a 'clean' form and not a document that was used for another client. The lawyer who sends an electronic document should be aware that the electronic document may be received or distributed to a person who is not a lawyer and who therefore does not have the duties of a recipient lawyer with respect to such document.

When removing or restricting access to metadata in documents produced or disclosed in litigation, the lawyer must take care not to violate any duty of disclosure to which the lawyer or the lawyer's client is subject. For a recent discussion relating to the duty to preserve and disclose metadata in a litigation context, *see Wyeth v. Impax Laboratories, Inc.*, 2006 WL 3091331 (D. Del. October 26, 2006). See also the Arizona Supreme Court's order dated September 5, 2007, on rule-change petition R-06-0034 (amending, effective January 1, 2008, the Arizona Rules of Civil Procedure to include provisions relating to discovery and disclosure of 'electronically stored information')."

D.C. Ethics Op. 341 (nonlitigation setting)	"Lawyers sending electronic documents outside of the context of responding to discovery or subpoenas have an obligation under Rule 1.6 to take reasonable steps to maintain the confidentiality of documents in their possession. This includes taking care to avoid providing electronic documents that inadvertently contain accessible information that is either a confidence or a secret and to employ reasonably available technical means to remove such metadata before sending the document. *See* N.Y. State Bar Ass'n Committee Op. 782. Accordingly, lawyers must either acquire sufficient understanding of the software that they use or ensure that their office employs safeguards to minimize the risk of inadvertent disclosures."
Florida Ethics Op. 06-2	"In order to maintain confidentiality under Rule 4-1.6(a), Florida lawyers must take reasonable steps to protect confidential information in all types of documents and information that leave the lawyers' offices, including electronic documents and electronic communications with other lawyers and third parties."
Maryland Ethics Op. 2007-09	"Absent an agreement with the receiving lawyer, based on Maryland RPC 1.1 and 1.6, 'the sending attorney has an ethical obligation to take reasonable measures to avoid the disclosure of confidential or work product materials imbedded in the electronic discovery.'"[1]
New York Ethics Op. 782	"The Lawyer's Code of Professional Responsibility (the 'Code') prohibits lawyers from 'knowingly' revealing a client confidence or secret, DR 4-101(B)(1), except when permitted under one of five exceptions enumerated in DR 4-101(C). DR 4-101(D) states that a lawyer 'shall exercise reasonable care to prevent his or her employees, associates, and others whose services are utilized by the lawyer from disclosing or

[1] The Maryland Committee added that not every inadvertent disclosure of privileged or work product material would constitute a violation of Rules 1.1 and 1.6, "since each case would have to be evaluated based on the facts and circumstances applicable hereto." Ethics Docket 2007-09.

using confidences or secrets of a client.' See also EC 4-5 ('Care should be exercised by a lawyer to prevent the disclosure of the confidences and secrets of one client to another'). Similarly, a lawyer who uses technology to communicate with clients must use reasonable care with respect to such communication, and therefore must assess the risks attendant to the use of that technology and determine if the mode of transmission is appropriate under the circumstances. *See* N.Y. State 709 (1998) ('an attorney must use reasonable care to protect confidences and secrets'); N.Y. City 94-11 (lawyer must take reasonable steps to secure client confidences or secrets).

When a lawyer sends a document by e-mail, as with any other type of communication, a lawyer must exercise reasonable care to ensure that he or she does not inadvertently disclose his or her client's confidential information. What constitutes reasonable care will vary with the circumstances, including the subject matter of the document, whether the document was based on a 'template' used in another matter for another client, whether there have been multiple drafts of the document with comments from multiple sources, whether the client has commented on the document, and the identity of the intended recipients of the document. Reasonable care may, in some circumstances, call for the lawyer to stay abreast of technological advances and the potential risks in transmission in order to make an appropriate decision with respect to the mode of transmission. *See* N.Y. State 709 (1998)."

New York County Lawyers' Association Opinion 738	(Nonlitigation only): "A lawyer who sends opposing counsel correspondence, contracts, or other similar documents electronically—as is now often the case—has the burden to take due care in appropriately scrubbing documents prior to sending them outside of the office or in sending them in a way that otherwise ensures that the documents are free of metadata."

APPENDIX III

Links to Opinions on Outsourcing

1. The State Bar of California Standing Committee on Professional Responsibility and Conduct, Formal Opinion No. 2004-165, https://www.lexisnexis.com/applieddiscovery/LawLibrary/CourtRulesArticles/CAstatebarop.pdf.
2. Los Angeles County Bar Association Professional and Ethics Committee Opinion No. 518 (June 19, 2006), http://www.lacba.org/Files/Main%20Folder/Documents/%20Ethics%20%20%20Opinions/Files/Ethics_Opinion_518.pdf.
3. San Diego County Bar Association Ethics Opinion 2007-1, http://www.sdcba.org/ethics/ethicsopinion07-1.htm.
4. The Association of Bar of the City of New York Committee on Professional and Judicial Ethics Formal Opinion 2006-3 (August 2006), http://www.nycbar.org/Ethics/eth2006.htm.
5. Professional Ethics of the Florida Bar Ethics Opinion 07-2 (January 18, 2008), http://www.floridabar.org/TFB/TFBResources.nsf/Attachments/DB3E4EDA068D9173852573530070B8D0/$FILE/07-2%20pao.pdf?OpenElement.

APPENDIX IV

Illinois State Bar Association Ethics Opinions Cited That Are Not Available Online to the General Public

ISBA Committee on Professional Conduct Opinion No. 01-01 (July 2001)

Topic: Lawyer's files; access to files stored on law firm's computer

Digest: When a former client is entitled to receive file material from a law firm, a law firm may not refuse a request to download onto disk such former client file materials stored on its computer system when such downloading can be accomplished easily and without disclosing the confidences of the firm's other clients.

Ref.: Illinois Rules of Professional Conduct 1.4(a); 1.6(a); and 1.15(b) Illinois Supreme Court Rules 201(b)(1) and 214; ISBA Advisory Opinion Nos. 94-13; 94-14; and 95-2; ABA Formal Ethics Opinion No. 99-414.

FACTS

Attorney Jones leaves the ABC law firm (ABC) in June 2000. Clients of Attorney Jones have written letters to ABC, stating that they wish their client file materials, including any generated, stored or archived on computer, to be transferred to Attorney Jones. Any outstanding legal fees have been paid. ABC law firm packs up Attorney Jones' files and sends them to Attorney Jones at his new law firm. Before those files were sent, ABC did not undertake to search its computer for client materials, nor did the firm undertake any comparison of documents on computer with the file materials put in boxes and sent over to Attorney Jones. The only overture the ABC law firm has made to the clients is to have Attorney Jones go through the boxes and see what documents are, or may be, missing. The ABC law firm would then make an attempt to search the firm's computer to see about the whereabouts of those particular documents. (Attorney Jones has no access to ABC's computer). Attorney Jones has requested that the ABC law firm merely download onto disk(s) all the client(s) file materials and then Attorney Jones would compare what is on the disk(s) to what is contained in the boxes. To download client file materials is easy to accomplish and client file materials on computer are accessed by attorney ID number, attorney initials and/or client name. The ABC law firm refuses to turn over client materials on computer to date.

QUESTION

Is a law firm obligated to download client files from its computer system and provide them to a former partner of the firm, per the clients' request, in order to ascertain that the client has received all documents to which the client is entitled?

OPINION

The principal rules governing a lawyer or law firm's duty to provide information and documents or other material to a client are Rules 1.4(a) and 1.15(b) of the Illinois Rules of Professional Conduct.

Rule 1.4(a) provides:

> A lawyer shall keep a client reasonably informed about the status of a matter and promptly comply with reasonable requests for information.

Rule 1.15(b) provides:

> Upon receiving funds or other property in which a client or third person has an interest, a lawyer shall promptly notify the client or third person. Except as stated in this rule or otherwise permitted by law or by agreement with the client, a lawyer shall promptly deliver to the client or third person any funds or other property that the client or third person is entitled to receive and, upon request by the client or third person, shall promptly render a full accounting regarding such property.

Therefore, a client cannot be denied access to his or her files, as this Committee stated in ISBA Opinion No. 95-02. The Rules of Professional Conduct, however, do not specify the format in which the client must be provided with his or her files. In light of modern business practices in this era of rapidly developing technology, the Committee believes it is important to address a law firm's obligation to provide its clients or former clients with files maintained on its computer system.

ISBA Opinion No. 94-13 has reviewed in detail seven categories of materials normally maintained in a client's file and evaluated the lawyer's duty to turn over or disclose each separate category of material, the issue of which of the clients' documents must be provided to the clients is not addressed herein. For purposes of this Opinion, it is noteworthy that the Committee concluded in ISBA Opinion No. 94-13 that a client is not entitled to an attorney's work product, including the attorney's notes, internal memoranda, legal research and factual research materials.

In the fact inquiry presented, the ABC law firm sent Attorney Jones his files without undertaking to search its computer for client materials, nor did the ABC law firm compare the documents it provided to Attorney Jones with those stored on its computer system. Although the Rules of Professional Conduct are silent as to whether the ABC law firm has any obligation to do so, the Illinois Supreme Court rules governing discovery are instructive. Rule 201(b)(1) defines the word "documents" to include "papers, photographs, films, recordings, memoranda, books, records, accounts, communications and all retrievable information in computer storage." The Committee Comments note that the definition of "documents" was expanded to include "all retrievable information in computer storage" in recognition of the "increasing reliability on computer technology." Thus, the Committee Comments conclude, a party is obligated to "produce on paper those relevant materials which have been stored electronically." Likewise, Supreme Court Rule 214, which governs document discovery, requires "a party to include in that party's production response all responsive information in computer storage in printed form." Committee Comments, Rule 214. The Committee Comments to Rule 214 further note "that there can be no question but that a producing party must search its computer storage when responding to a request to produce documents pursuant to this rule." While discovery rules do not control issues of professional conduct, both sets of rules are promulgated by the Illinois Supreme Court, and should therefore be interpreted in a consistent manner. Under the facts presented, it is the Committee's opinion that the ABC law firm must download Attorney Jones's client file materials onto disks.

It is also the Committee's opinion that the request to have client file materials downloaded onto disk is a "reasonable" request as set forth in Rule 1.4(a), and that the client is entitled to receive his or her files in the format in which the lawyer or law firm maintains such files. Moreover, as the facts represent that downloading client file materials is easy to accomplish, it would be far more efficient and cost-effective to proceed in this manner rather than to require Attorney Jones to search through the boxes in order to figure out what documents may be missing. Although the expense which would be incurred in downloading the client file materials is likely to be minimal, as set forth in ISBA Opinion No. 94-14, the ABC law firm may be entitled to compensation for the reasonable expense involved in retrieving the files in question and providing on disk copies of materials that were already provided to Attorney Jones and his clients.

Moreover, under the facts presented, there are no confidentiality concerns, which would warrant the ABC law firm's refusal to download the client files onto disks. Rule 1.6(a) provides that "a lawyer shall not, during or after termination of the professional relationship with the client, use or reveal a confidence or secret of the client known to the lawyer unless the client consents after disclosure." While it is certainly true that there would be information on the law firm's other client files stored on the computer that would constitute a confidence or secret of the other clients, the fact inquiry states that client file materials on the ABC law firm's computer are accessed by attorney i.d. number, attorney initials and/or client name. Accordingly, the ABC law firm could download only Attorney Jones's client files without fear of disclosing the confidences of its other clients.

* * *

Illinois State Bar Association Opinion No. 94-14 (January 1995)

Topic: Lawyer's Files; Duty to Return client papers.

Digest: Upon termination of representation, a lawyer is required to return all papers and property received from the client, but may retain copies at the lawyer's expense. If the client requests copies of other parts of the lawyer's file, the lawyer should make copies of those materials in the lawyer's file to which the client is entitled to access available at the client's expense.

Ref: Illinois Rules of Professional Conduct, Rules 1.4, 1.6, 1.15 and 1.16. ISBA Opinion No. 94-13 (1995).

FACTS

The inquiring lawyer served as village attorney for a Village for thirty years prior to retirement. Upon retirement, the lawyer turned over all active files to his successor. Recently, the Village Administrator has asked the lawyer to turn over all files, both active and inactive. Most of the files are now in storage, together with files of clients from the lawyer's former and present law firm. The lawyer believes that the Village Administrator's request is overly broad and burdensome. To alleviate the burden, the Village Administrator has offered to send someone to the lawyer's storage facility to assist in sorting and pulling the relevant files.

QUESTIONS

1. Is the Village Administrator entitled to both the lawyer's active and inactive files?
2. If the Village Administrator is entitled to both active and inactive files, who bears the cost of copying the files?
3. If the lawyer were to permit the Village Administrator's personnel to assist in pulling and sorting files, would this breach the lawyer's obligation to protect and maintain the secrets and confidence of other clients?

OPINION

1. It appears that the Village has in effect discharged the lawyer and the designated successor. This situation is treated as a withdrawal from representation under the Illinois Rules of Professional Conduct. Rule 1.16(d) provides in relevant part: "A lawyer shall not withdraw from employment until the lawyer has taken reasonable steps to avoid foreseeable prejudice to the rights of the client, including . . . delivering to the client all papers and property to which the client is entitled."

   Generally, a lawyer may retain a client's papers or property only if asserting a common law or statutory retaining lien. In the facts presented, the lawyer has not suggested that any fee is owed relating to representation of the Village. Accordingly, there does not appear to be a retaining lien on the Village's files.

   In its recent Opinion No. 94-13, the Committee discussed the lawyer's duty under Rule 1.4(a) and Rule 1.15(b) to provide copies of and access to the various types of material usually contained in a lawyer's files. In general, the client is entitled under Rule 1.15(b) to the return of all materials that the client has provided to the lawyer; and the lawyer's obligation extends to both active and inactive files. Similarly, the client's right to access to other types of file material extends to both active and inactive files.
2. As noted above, Opinion No. 94-13 reviewed in detail the types of materials normally maintained in a lawyer's file and evaluated the lawyer's duty to turn over or disclose each separate category of material. All original papers delivered to the lawyer by the client must be returned to the client. The lawyer may make copies of such material, if desired, at the lawyer's expense.

With respect to other parts of the lawyer's file to which the client is entitled to access, including copies of documents that the client has already received, the originals may be retained by the lawyer and the client should be permitted to have copies at the client's expense. Consistent with Opinion No. 94-13, the Committee does not believe that a lawyer is required to act as a storage facility for clients, and therefore the lawyer is entitled to compensation for the reasonable expense involved in retrieving the files in question and providing copies of materials that the client has already received. The lawyer is also entitled to compensation for the reasonable expense of providing copies of any materials, such as routine administrative correspondence with third parties, that the client may not have received because the lawyer had no duty to provide the client with copies of such materials in the normal course of the representation, but to which the client is entitled to access upon reasonable request.

3. Rule 1.6(a) provides that a lawyer generally shall not, either during or after termination of the professional relationship with the client, use or reveal a confidence or secret of the client, unless the client consents after disclosure. Clearly there would be information on the lawyer's other files in storage that would constitute a confidence or secret of the other clients, whether it be the client's name, address, or a labeling of the subject matter. Assuming that the lawyer does not obtain the consent of every current or former client for whom there is a file in storage, allowing personnel from the Village to sort through those files would violate Rule 1.6. As noted in Opinion No. 94-13, the lawyer may charge the reasonable expense of locating and copying those parts of the lawyer's file that the client has not provided, but to which the client is entitled to access.

INDEX

ABOUT THE AUTHOR

John M. Barkett

Mr. Barkett is a partner at the law firm of Shook, Hardy & Bacon L.L.P., in its Miami office. He is a graduate of the University of Notre Dame (B.A. Government, 1972, *summa cum laude)* and the Yale Law School (J.D., 1975), and served as a law clerk to the Honorable David W. Dyer on the old Fifth Circuit Court of Appeals. Mr. Barkett is an adjunct professor of law at the University of Miami Law School.

Mr. Barkett has, over the years, been a commercial litigator (contract and corporate disputes, employment, trademark, and antitrust), environmental litigator (CERCLA, RCRA, and toxic tort), and, for the past several years, a peacemaker and problem solver, serving as an arbitrator, mediator, facilitator, or allocator in a variety of environmental or commercial contexts. He is a certified mediator under the rules of the Supreme Court of Florida, serves on the CPR Institute for Dispute Resolution's "Panel of Distinguished Neutrals," and is on the National Roster of Environmental Dispute Resolution and Consensus Building Professionals maintained by the U.S. Institute for Environmental Conflict Resolution. He has served or is serving as a neutral in more than fifty matters involving in the aggregate more than $450 million. He has conducted or is conducting arbitrations under the rules of CPR, AAA rules, and the LCIA. In November 2003, he was appointed by the presiding judge to serve as the Special Master to oversee the implementation and enforcement of the 1992 Consent Decree between the United States and the State of Florida relating to the restoration of the Florida Everglades. He also consults with major corporations on the evaluation of legal strategy and risk and conducts independent investigations where such services are needed.

Mr. Barkett is a Fellow of the American College of Environmental Lawyers. He also serves on the Council of the ABA Section of Litigation after service as the Section's co-director of CLE and co-chair of the Environmental Litigation Committee.

Mr. Barkett is editor and one of the authors of the Section of Litigation's Monograph, EX PARTE CONTACTS WITH FORMER EMPLOYEES (Environmental Litigation Committee, October 2002). His paper, *A Baker's Dozen: Reasons Why You Should Read the 2002 Model Rules of Professional Conduct*, was presented at the Section of Litigation's 2003 Annual Conference. Mr. Barkett also wrote *The MJP Maze: Avoiding the Unauthorized Practice of Law*, which was presented at the 2005 Section of

Litigation Annual Conference. He also wrote *Refresher Ethics: Conflicts of Interest*, for the Section's January 2007 Joint Environmental, Products Liability, and Mass Torts CLE program, and *Tattletales or Crimestoppers: Disclosure Ethics Under Model Rules 1.6 and 1.13*, presented at the ABA Annual Meeting (Atlanta, August 7, 2004) and, in an updated version, at the ABA Tort and Insurance Practice Section Spring CLE Meeting (Phoenix, April 11, 2008). Mr. Barkett also presented his paper, *From Canons to Cannon*, at the Ethics Centennial sponsored by the ABA Section of Litigation (Washington, D.C. April 18, 2008) commemorating the 100th anniversary of the adoption of the Canons of Ethics.

Mr. Barkett is also the author of Ethical Issues in Environmental Dispute Resolution, a chapter in the ABA publication, Environmental Dispute Resolution, An Anthology of Practical Experience (July 2002), *Tipping the Scales of Justice: The Rise of ADR* 22 NRE 40 (2008) and *The Pieces to the Privilege Protection Puzzle*, 22 N.R.E. 50 (2007).

Mr. Barkett has published one book on e-discovery, *E-Discovery: Twenty Questions and Answers*, (First Chair Press, Chicago, October 2008). He has also published or presented a number of articles in the e-discovery arena:

- *Bytes, Bits and Bucks: Cost-Shifting and Sanctions in E-Discovery*, ABA Section of Litigation Annual Meeting (2004) and 71 Def. Couns. J. 334 (2004).
- *The Prelitigation Duty to Preserve: Lookout!*, ABA Annual Meeting, Chicago (2005).
- *Help Is On The Way . . . Sort Of: How the Civil Rules Advisory Committee Hopes to Fill the E-Discovery Void*, ABA Section of Litigation Annual Meeting, Los Angeles (2006)
- *Help Has Arrived . . . Sort Of: The New E-Discovery Rules*, ABA Section of Litigation Annual Meeting, San Antonio (2007)
- *The Battle For Bytes: New Rule 26*, e-Discovery (Section of Litigation, February 2006).
- *E-Discovery For Arbitrators*, 1 Dispute Resolution International Journal 129 (International Bar Association, December 2007).

In the fall of 2007, Mr. Barkett taught a first-ever course at the University of Miami Law School entitled, "E-Discovery."

Among his other works are a terrorism-related article on torts, entitled, *If Terror Reigns, Will Torts Follow?* 9 Widener Law Symposium 485 (2003); *A Database Analysis of the Superfund Allocation Case Law* (Shook, Hardy & Bacon L.L.P., Miami, 2003); and *The CERCLA Limitations Puzzle*, 19 N.R.E. 70 (2004).

Mr. Barkett recently has been recognized in the areas of alternative dispute resolution and environmental law in a number of lawyer-recognition publications, including Who's Who Legal (International Bar Association, since 2005); Best Lawyers in America (National Law Journal, since 2005); Legal Elite (Florida Trend, since 2004), and Chambers USA America's Leading Lawyers (since 2004). Mr. Barkett can be reached at jbarkett@shb.com.